THE
BASIC
COOKBOOK
2ND EDITION

Notices

IBM PC is a registered trademark of International Business Machines Corp.
Commodore 64 is a registered trademark of Commodore Electronics Ltd.
TRS-80 is a trademark of the Radio Shack Division of Tandy Corporation.
Apple is a registered trademark of Apple Computer, Inc.

No. 1855
$12.95

THE
BASIC
COOKBOOK
2ND EDITION

**KEN TRACTON &
THOMAS A. WELLS**

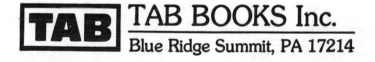

TAB BOOKS Inc.
Blue Ridge Summit, PA 17214

SECOND EDITION

FIRST PRINTING

Copyright © 1985 by TAB BOOKS Inc.

Printed in the United States of America

Library of Congress Cataloging in Publication Data

Tracton, Ken.
   The BASIC cookbook.

   Includes index.
   1. Basic (Computer program language) I. Wells,
Thomas A. II. Title.
QA76.73.B3T7 1985   001.64'.24   84-26896
ISBN 0-8306-0855-9
ISBN 0-8306-1855-4 (pbk.)

Contents

Derived Functions—Diagnostics (Common)—Increase Program Speed—Saving Space—Speed (Processing)

Preface

The revisions to *The BASIC Cookbook* were made to make it more current in today's world of microcomputers. With more microcomputers on the market, more versions of BASIC have appeared. Not all of these versions use the same keywords; some versions omit some keywords, and others use the same keyword differently, or different keywords for the same result.

In an effort to clarify the uses of the keywords, additional definitions are included in the main part of the book, programming examples have been revised and new ones added, and all the examples have been reviewed and changed as needed to make sure they will run on many different kinds of microcomputers, such as the IBM PC, Commodore 64, TRS-80, and Apple.

Further changes include expanded explanations for some of the keyword definitions to clarify those that may have been too brief in the original edition, or for any whose usage may have changed over the years.

Finally, additions were made to the definitions to help programmers find ways of simulating a keyword, if their version of BASIC does not have a particular keyword or function.

Introduction

WHAT IS A COMPUTER?

Think of a computer as a super-duper calculator. If you just turn the calculator on, nothing will happen. In order for a calculator to operate, you must feed in numbers and operations. An *operation* is an instruction to your calculator to perform a function: add, divide, find the square root, etc. For a computer, however, we must also instruct the computer to accept the numbers and to perform the operations.

If computers could work only with numbers, we would not need them; programmable calculators would be adequate for almost all our calculation needs. However, a computer can also work on *alphanumerics,* which are all the characters on your keyboard: the letters, the numbers, the punctuation marks and the signs above the numbers.

WHAT IS A PROGRAM?

A *program* may be defined as a set of directions that tell a computer how to solve a problem. Any program may be considered to have three parts:

1. The necessary information, the *input data*.
2. The processing of the input data.
3. The *output*, results obtained from the processing.

These instructions must be written in a language which is understood by the computer.

Of all the high-level computer languages that have been written since 1955, BASIC (Beginner's All-purpose Symbolic Instruction Code) is definitely one of the easiest to learn. The simplicity of this language is actually quite deceiving as it possesses sufficient power and flexibility to solve a wide variety of problems. BASIC is available on most time-sharing large computer systems as well as being the number one language of the microcomputers.

The instructions in BASIC resemble algebraic formulae and include English statements. Since its structure is well suited for algebraic manipulation, BASIC is very useful for problem solving in science, mathematics, and engineering; but it is also used in many areas of numeric or character manipulation, such as medicine, psychology, economics, and business.

BASIC AS A CALCULATOR

Most versions of BASIC have a type of operation called *direct entry*. If you enter an operation without a line number, the operation is performed immediately and the answer is printed if the word PRINT precedes the operation.

The following are examples of direct entry and your fundamental functions. The first statement is your one line program; the number below is the computer output.

PRINT 5 + 6
11

PRINT 7*11
77

PRINT 39/13
3

PRINT SIN (.785398)
0.7071

PRINT LOG (20)
2.99573

```
PRINT SQR (2)
1.41421

PRINT 23*34.8
800.4

PRINT INT (45/8)
5

PRINT ABS (−9)
9

PRINT RND (0)
0.9463

PRINT RND (0)
0.2166
```

Note that each call to RND (0) will produce a uniquely different random number. For further explanation of this function, look up *RND*.

These fundamental operations may be combined to produce complex results with ease. When combining operations, all expressions follow standard computer hierarchy of operations, and the computer will calculate:

> First: Exponentiation ↑ or ▲ (in some basics **)
> Second: Multiplication *
>   Division /
> Third: Addition +
>   Subtraction −

When two operators belong to the same group,

> Example: 5 + 3 − 4
>   6*7/2

the computer reads from left to right and performs the operations from left to right.

Example: (5 + 3) − 4
(6 * 7)/2

Parentheses are often used to control the order in which the computer evaluates combined expressions. When this is done, the computer evaluates the innermost expression first, then the next, and so on.

Your computer may use a different sequence for evaluating expressions; likely there are more operations listed than the few fundamental ones just listed. To locate the list for your computer, look under the keyword *hierarchy* in this book and your computer's reference manual.

HOW DO I WRITE A PROGRAM?

A complete BASIC program consists of an ordered sequence of statements, each instruction being written as a separate statement. These statements *must* appear in the order in which they are to be executed unless a deliberate transfer of control is indicated, for example, a subroutine.

The following rules always apply:

1) Every statement must appear on a separate line, unless the version allows multiline statements.
2) A statement cannot exceed one line in length, unless the version of BASIC being used has multi-line statements.
3) Each statement must begin with a positive integer quantity, called the statement number or line number.
4) No two statements may have the same line number.
5) Successive statements must have increasing (ascending) line numbers.
6) Each statement must contain a BASIC keyword, except versions of BASIC which do not require the LET keyword.
7) Blank spaces may be inserted anywhere desired in order to improve the readability of the statements.

Now let us examine a program named GUESS, written in BASIC that illustrates the fundamental concepts in this language. This program was chosen primarily because it contains no "bells or whistles" belonging to a SUPER BASIC program. The more esoteric statements and commands are covered in detail elsewhere in this text.

A BASIC PROGRAM

LOAD,GUESS
READY
LIST

```
10      REM THIS PROGRAM DEMONSTRATES BASIC
20      REM THE LINES 30 AND 40 ASK FOR A RANDOM
            NUMBER
30      PRINT "ENTER ANY NUMBER FROM 1 TO 100"
40      INPUT X
50      REM LINE 60 EVALUATES A RANDOM NUMBER
60      X = INT(X*RND (0))
70      REM THE FOLLOWING LINES ACCEPT THE GUESSES
80      PRINT "YOUR GUESS IS";
90      INPUT Y
100     IF Y = X THEN 200
110     IF Y>X THEN 300
120     PRINT "YOUR GUESS IS TOO LOW"
130     GOTO 80
200     PRINT "YOU HAVE GUESSED   CORRECTLY THE
            RANDOM NUMBER"
210     STOP
300     PRINT "YOUR GUESS IS TOO HIGH"
310     GOTO 80
320     END
READY
RUN
ENTER ANY NUMBER FROM 1 TO 100
? 50
YOUR GUESS IS ? 65
YOUR GUESS IS TOO LOW
YOUR GUESS IS ? 100
YOUR GUESS IS TOO HIGH
YOUR GUESS IS ? 75
YOUR GUESS IS TOO LOW
YOUR GUESS IS ? 80
YOU HAVE GUESSED CORRECTLY THE RANDOM NUMBER
END
```

Let us look at what has happened, and how this program in
BASIC operated. We started with the *command* LOAD,GUESS
which instructed the computer to search its library for the program
named GUESS. Where the program was stored is not of impor-
tance; it may have been on disc or on tape. Once the stored program was found, it was transferred to the main memory of the
computer.

When the computer was ready to accept another command it

printed READY. A computer, while very fast, can only do one operation at a time. When it is free from a task it will notify the user by some message, usually the words GO, OK, or READY. We next typed in the command LIST, which instructed the computer to print out the program now residing under the name "GUESS" in main memory.

Notice that although we haven't said it directly, there is a special key used to inform the computer that we have issued a command. It is called the "ENTER" key, or sometimes the "RETURN" key, and it is pressed after each command has been typed in. In this example, when the computer displayed the READY message, we typed in the command LIST. Nothing happens though, until we press the ENTER key.

As soon as the ENTER key is pressed, the computer begins to list the program. The same is true of any command we might use, such as RUN, LOAD, or LIST.

We list a program to verify that we have entered the right program instructions or to make corrections to an already written program. We do not have to list a program first to RUN it. After the computer had listed the program GUESS, it again printed the READY message to indicate that it was waiting for a user command.

Typing the command RUN instructed the computer to start processing the program.

Looking through the program we notice the words REM at lines 10, 20, 50 and 70. The REM statement allows the programmer to add *REM*arks to a program. Whenever the computer reads a line beginning with the word REM, it does not process that line. Only during listing is a REM line evaluated.

One purpose of the REM statement is to enable the user to add useful information concerning the program when it is read or listed in the future. Quite often in long programs a user will forget why he wrote a certain line in a certain fashion. The REM removes this problem. Of course the REM statement is also useful for users other than the original programmer who wish to understand what a certain line does.

In line 30 we notice the word PRINT. The PRINT statement prints all characters that are enclosed in quotation marks following the word PRINT. The PRINT statement thus allows the program to output information, words or numbers. Whenever we wish to print anything in BASIC we use the PRINT statement.

The INPUT statement in line 40 tells the computer to ask for a number and assign the number then given by the user to the variable named X in this case. In line 90 the number is assigned to the variable Y. The INPUT statement allows us to *input* or enter information into the computer.

Line 60 X = INT (X*RND 0) constructed a random number from the number entered by the user in line 40. The word RND (0) is an instruction which tells the computer to pick a random number from 0 to 1 such as 0.96784. We then multiplied the number we entered by the random number. Since we are only interested in having an integer number in this program, we used the INT instruction which tells the computer to only use the integer part of a number. The resulting random integer number is assigned to the variable X. Whenever we assign a number to a variable that has been already used, the former number is lost.

In lines 100 and 110 we test to see if the number entered as a guess is in fact the random number. Line 100 tests whether the number is equal or not. If it is equal, we branch or go to line 200. If the test is false, Y is greater or less than X, and the next line, 110, is executed. Line 110 checks whether the number is greater than X. If it is, we go to line 300; if it is not, the next line is executed and prints a message saying we are too low in our guess. If Y = X and line 200 were executed, the "correct" message would be printed, and the next line encountered would be the STOP instruction which instructs the computer to stop program execution and END.

The END statement at the "end" of the program in line 320 tells the computer that this is the end of the program and that it should stop execution and await another user command.

The following list will give you some idea of the terms common to BASIC programming. Be sure to look them up in this book and in your computer's guide to become familiar with their meaning and usage.

It should be obvious by now that the *execution* of the lines is sequential, going from lowest line number to highest line number. The only mechanisms that have disturbed this flow are the GOTO, and THEN instructions in lines 100, 110, 130 and 310.

The user may try this "basic" BASIC program and get the feel for this language. Reading the text the reader will find that writing in BASIC is much simpler than he expected. It is definitely "people-oriented." It does not require an extensive training in mathematics or programming.

BASIC programs are also very easy to alter. Once written, a

program may be easily modified to suit other applications.

Because most BASICs are so similar, a program written on one machine will usually run on another computer, except for a few minor differences that may exist from one version to the next.

GOOD PRACTICE HINTS IN BASIC

1) Use REMs for documentation whenever possible.
2) Increment line number by 10, leaving space for future updates.
3) Write only one statement per line.
4) Try to avoid the special features available only on your version of BASIC.
5) Use I, J, K for index or counting variables throughout the program.
6) Use L, M, N for the end points or loops (FOR I = 1 TO M).
7) Avoid the letter O as a variable as confusion is inevitable with zero, whether your computer slashes the letter O or the zero.
8) Unless tight for space, do not reuse variable names.

BASIC AND COMPUTER SYSTEMS

BASIC is usually run on computers that operate in one of the following three modes:

A) Stand-alone
B) Time-sharing
C) BATCH

Stand-Alone

In the stand-alone mode the computer is dedicated to only one user. That is, only one job or program is being run until completion. Generally the large computer systems are not stand-alone as it is not economically feasible to dedicate a large system to a single user.

Typical single-user machines are the host of microcomputers now available, and some of the specialized minicomputers.

The advantage, of course, of single-user, stand-alone operation is that the user has full command of the computer.

Time-Sharing

In the time-sharing mode the computer is used "simultaneously" by more than one user. Each user can communicate with the computer via an input/output terminal which may be a teleprinter, video terminal or a combination of both.

The program and data are entered via the user's terminal and the results are returned to that terminal after processing.

There are many ways time-sharing may be effected by a computer. The system may take advantage of the slow response time of terminals and process data while the terminals are transmitting or receiving information. The system may also time-slice the users; that is, each user is allotted a time slot, and is polled in a round-robin method. Each user may be given 100 milliseconds of computer time, for example, then the next, and the next, and so on, until the computer returns to the original user. If the time slots are small and there are few users, each user views the system as being dedicated solely to his job.

Batch Mode

In the BATCH mode a number of jobs (programs) are entered into the computer and are processed sequentially. Typically this operational mode is done with punched cards, with both the program and data being recorded on these cards. A punched card typically contains 80 columns, of which some or all may contain holes. The pattern of holes in each column encodes the data, information, or instructions. Since each column represents one character, a single card can hold up to 80 characters of information. The cards are punched on special "card punches," then read into the computer by a card-reading device. The output of the program will then be printed on a line printer or, if graphics are being handled, on a plotter.

The advantage of the BATCH mode is that extremely large programs and quantities of data can be transmitted into and out of the computer very quickly. Therefore the BATCH mode is well suited for jobs that require large quantities of computer processing time or are physically long in length.

The serious drawback is that even if a given program requires only a few seconds of computer time, it may be resident within the system for a few hours to many days. Each job must wait until its turn has come up. Jobs are served on a first-in, first-to-be-processed basis. Thus for simple jobs the BATCH method is definitely undesirable.

THE AVAILABILITY OF BASIC

BASIC is now available as a compiler, translator, or interpreter. An interpreter stores in memory exactly what the user has entered. Upon execution the interpreter scans each line of code, translates the code into computer machine language (the fundamental machine codes the particular computer understands) and then executes the machine language image of the line. This sequence must be done for each line. Whether any given line has been interpreted once already is unimportant. The language does not store the machine code image. Thus in the even of a line being used ten times, it must be interpreted ten times.

A translator stores not the entered lines but rather a coded version of the input material. This coded version must still be interpreted but, because it is coded by function, it saves space and offers an increase in speed. Whether for interpretation or translation, the full BASIC language package must reside in memory.

A compiler compiles or "images" the total program as opposed to line by line into machine code. Thus, even if a line is used ten times it is only compiled once. The total compiled image is stored in memory and is called an object program as opposed to a source program, which is the original material. A compiler offers dramatic speed increases, and only requires a portion of the language package to remain in memory. This portion of compiler BASIC is called the run-time module. The run-time module effectively executes the BASIC compiled program.

The ability to run the same BASIC program on different machines is because, whether the version of BASIC is a translator, interpreter, or compiler, the end result is machine language. A version of BASIC written for one machine will use the instruction set of that computer to duplicate the functions of a BASIC written for another computer (machine language programs cannot be transferred from computer to computer).

If you're unfamiliar with BASIC programming, the entries listed below will give you a working knowledge of the language:

Argument	Hierarchy
Array	INPUT
Assignment	INT
CLEAR	Library Functions
Conditional Branching	Line Numbers
COS	LIST

END	Loops
Files	MARGIN
FOR-TO	Multiline Functions
GOSUB	Multiple Branching
GOTO	Nested Loops
NOT	RUN
Numbers	SCRATCH
ON GO-SUB	SGN
OR	SIN
PI	SPACE$
PRINT	SQR
PRINT USING	STOP
Program	String
RANDOMIZE	Subroutine
REM	Subscripted Variables
RETURN	TAN
RND	Variables

This list gives (in capitals) about 28 BASIC keywords. Most current versions of BASIC have at least twice this number. The most complete versions can have 170 or even more keywords, which are commands or statements recognized by the computer as orders to do something specific.

The most important aid that a new (or even an experienced) BASIC programmer can have is the programmer's reference guide for the version of BASIC that is used by the computer being programmed. This guide, usually supplied by the computer manufacturer, must be used as the final authority when you are faced with the question "What does this keyword mean for this computer?". This book can help you understand, probably much better than the guide, the uses for each keyword.

The BASIC language now has literally scores of dialects differing from each other in minor, and sometimes, major ways. These differences occur in two ways: various keywords are used for the same commands or statements, or the same keywords may have varying uses—causing the computer to respond differently. This book can help you understand the differences and learn most of the fundamental keywords through examples and short programs.

A Dictionary
of BASIC Programming

● **ABS:** The library function ABS returns the absolute value of the expression within the parentheses that follow the keyword ABS.

EXAMPLES:

```
10    Y = ABS(J)
20    K = ABS(J−2)
30    PRINT ABS(A1)
```

PROGRAMMING EXAMPLE:

```
10    REM THIS PROGRAM DEMONSTRATES THE
20    REM ABS FUNCTION
30    PRINT "INPUT ANY NUMBER"
40    INPUT K
50    LET K = ABS(K)
60    PRINT LOG(K)
70    GOTO 30
80    END
```

RUN

INPUT ANY NUMBER
?-4
1.38629

1

2 ABS-AND

```
INPUT ANY NUMBER
?16
2.77259
INPUT ANY NUMBER
?-2563
7.84893

END
```

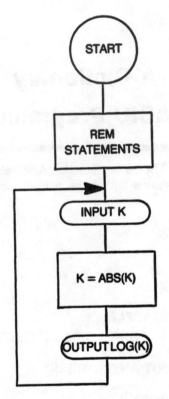

Flowchart for ABS function example.

● **AND:** The AND statement is a logical operator which relates two operands, one preceding the AND and one following. It can be used with two numeric or string variables or expressions.

When used with numeric operands, AND operates on them in binary fashion, converting each to binary and comparing them bit by bit. The result of the statement 5 AND 8, for example, is zero, since 5 is binary 0101 and 8 is binary 1000. For comparison, 7 AND 1 is one, since binary 7 is 0111 and binary 1 is 0001.

PROGRAMMING EXAMPLE:

```
10    REM THIS PROGRAM DEMONSTRATES THE
20    REM AND STATEMENT
30    LET K = 10
```

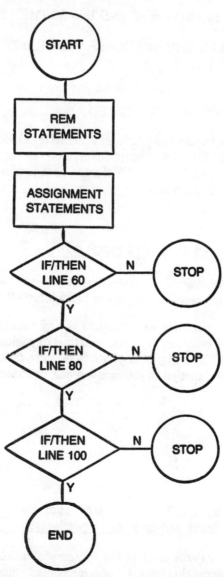

Flowchart for AND statement example.

4 AND-Array

```
40    LET J = 20
50    LET L = 30
60    IF K = J/2 AND L = K + J THEN 80
70    STOP
80    IF J = L - K AND J = K*2 THEN 100
90    STOP
100   IF K = 10 AND J = 20 AND L = 30 THEN 120
110   STOP
120 PRINT "ALL THE BRANCHES OCCURRED"
```

RUN

ALL THE BRANCHES OCCURRED

The AND statement may be used with the IF-THEN statement. It allows the IF-THEN statement to have two or more qualifiers instead of only one. The IF-THEN statement is true if and only if both qualifiers are true.

EXAMPLE:

```
10    IF X = 10 AND Y = 15 THEN 600
```

In the above example both the first qualifier (X = 10) and the second (Y = 15) must be true if the branch to 600 is to occur.

● **Argument:** An *argument* is any numeric or string quantity that is required by a mathematical or logical expression to operate on. The arguments of a function are those items that are used by the function to produce a result or evaluation of that function.

EXAMPLE:

1. SIN(X)
2. 2*3
3. A/B

In this example, X, 2, 3, A, and B are arguments of the functions sine, multiplication, and division, respectively.

● **Array:** A table or list of items is called an array. A list has only items that have a one-dimensional value, namely its position in the list relative to the first entry in the list. An array is a two-dimensional entity that has rows and columns; thus every item must have a row and a column value.

EXAMPLE:

LIST
3456.98
7856989
6756.09
6754444

This list has 4 items. Each item may be identified by its position in the list: 6756.09 is the third item in the list.

If we let the subscripted variable L represent the list, then L(1) equals 3456.98; L(2) equals 7856989, and so on. Telling the computer to PRINT L(3) will result in the value 6756.09 being printed on the screen.

How are the values put into the variable L? Use the assignment statement: LET L(1) = 3456.98. Do this for each of the values of the subscript, in this case 1 through 4. Then, unless you change these values later in the program, the list is stored safely in an array.

45	78	67	78
53	67	98	23
32	84	21	90
34	29	53	71

This table has numbers in four columns and four rows. Each item is identified by its row and column value. In the above example 67 is in the second row and the second column.

If the name of the table was A then A(2,2) would stand for 67, the element in the second row and in the second column of the array named A.

● **ASC:** The ASC library function converts any single character to its ASCII equivalent. Thus this function will usually accept a single character as an argument. One use of the ASC function is to permit alphabetization. As the code is in alphabetic sequence, we merely convert the characters to their ASCII values and compare them to find which is larger.

Some version of BASIC allow the argument to be entered directly as a letter or character, such as K = ASC(P). Other versions require the argument to be enclosed in double quotes, such as K = ASC("P"). Check your manual to determine which ver-

6 ASC

sion works on your computer.

A string variable may also usually be the argument of the ASC function, such as K = ASC(P\$), where the string variable P\$ has previously been assigned a value. If the string variable has a length of more than one—say you have assigned it this way: P\$ = "ABCD"—then the ASC function usually only returns the ASCII value of the first character of the string. In this case, the ASCII value of the letter A would be returned, and the values for B, C, and D would not be considered.

EXAMPLE:

```
10    LET A = ASC(Z)
20    LET B = ASC(P)
30    LET H = ASC(C)
40    LET J = ASC(K)

50  LET K = ASC("P")
60  LET N = ASC(H$)
```

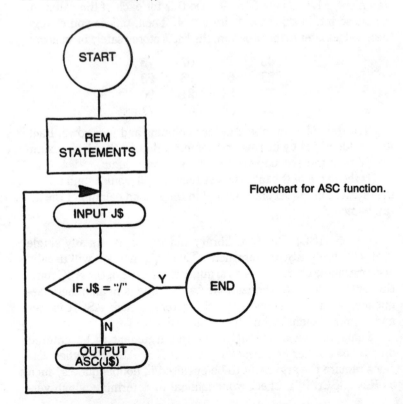

Flowchart for ASC function.

PROGRAMMING EXAMPLE:

```
10    REM THIS PROGRAM DEMONSTRATES
20    REM THE ASC FUNCTION
30    PRINT "INPUT A LETTER"
40    INPUT J$
50    IF J$ = "/" THEN 80
60    PRINT ASC (J$)
70    GOTO 30
80    END
```

RUN

INPUT A LETTER
?A
65
INPUT A LETTER
?K
75
INPUT A LETTER
?/

END

PROGRAMMING EXAMPLE:

```
10    REM THIS PROGRAM USES
20    REM THE ASC FUNCTION
30    PRINT "INPUT TWO LETTERS"
40    INPUT A$,B$
50    A = ASC(A$)
60    B = ASC(B$)
70    IF A>B THEN 110
80    IF A = B THEN 130
90    PRINT A$; "IS LESS THAN";B$
100   STOP
110   PRINT A$; "IS GREATER THAN";B$
120   STOP
130   PRINT A$; "IS EQUAL TO";B$
140   STOP
150   END
```

RUN
INPUT TWO LETTERS
?K,T
T IS GREATER THAN K

END

8 ASCII—Assignment

● **ASCII:** See *CHANGE*

● **Assignment:** The assignment statement assigns the value of a constant or a string to a variable. The value of the term on the right of the equal sign is assigned to the variable on the left.

EXAMPLES:

```
10    LET J = K-9
20    LET A2 = 365.25
30    LET Q$ = "HELLO"
40    LET K$ = J$
```

Similarly, we have

```
10    J = K-9
20    A2 = 365.25
30    Q$ = "HELLO" (Note: Strings must always be enclosed by
          quotation marks)
40    K$ = J$
```

The keyword LET is optional in most versions of BASIC.

An assignment statement does not correspond to an algebraic expression, for example:

```
10    J = J + 1
20    N = N*2
```

Assignment statements are always interpreted as carrying out the operations on the right and assigning the resulting value to the variable on the left. Thus the statement $J = J + 1$ is interpreted as, "Take the value of J, increment it by 1 and assign it to the variable J." Thereafter the variable J has a new value.

Note the difference between an assignment statement and an algebraic expression: the variable names of an assignment statement are different on each side of the equal sign, such as LET J = K + 1. In this statement, the value of the variable K, on the right side of the equal sign, is not changed when the computer executes the statement.

In an algebraic expression, the same variable name appears on both sides of the equal sign, such as LET J = J + 1. In this statement, the value of the variable J, on the right and left sides of the equal sign, is changed; the quantity 1 has been added to it.

PROGRAMMING EXAMPLE:

```
10    REM THIS PROGRAM DEMONSTRATES THE
20    REM ASSIGNMENT STATEMENT
30    REM ASSIGNMENT USING LET
```

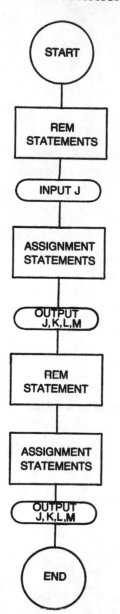

Flowchart for Assignment statement.

```
10    Assignment-ATN
40    PRINT "INPUT A NUMBER THAT IS POSITIVE"
50    INPUT J
60    LET K = J*2
70    LET L = LOG(J)
80    LET M = SIN(J)
90    PRINT J,K,L,M
100   REM ASSIGNMENT NOT USING LET
110   K = J/2
120   L = J*LOG(J)
130   M = J/SIN(J)
140   PRINT J,K,L,M
150   END
```

● **ATN:** The library function ATN returns the arctangent of the argument enclosed in parentheses. The result is returned in radians on most computers.

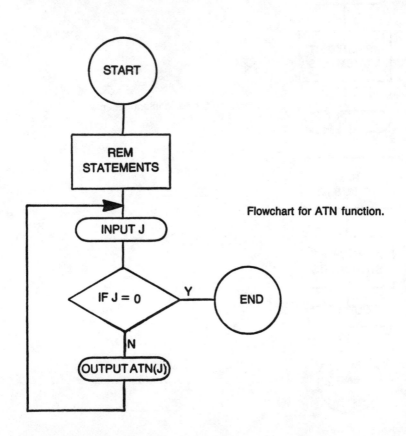

Flowchart for ATN function.

EXAMPLES:

```
10    PRINT ATN(X)
20    Z = ATN(X)
```

PROGRAMMING EXAMPLE:

```
10    REM THIS PROGRAM DEMONSTRATES
20    REM THE ATN FUNCTION
30    PRINT "INPUT A NUMBER"
40    INPUT J
50    IF J = 0 THEN 80
60    PRINT ATN(J)
70    GOTO 30
80    END
```

RUN

```
INPUT A NUMBER
?2
1.10715
INPUT A NUMBER
?3.14159
1.26263
INPUT A NUMBER
?1
0.78539
INPUT A NUMBER
?0
```

END

● **Back Slash:** See *Colon.*

● **BYE:** The BYE command, usually associated with large computer time-sharing systems returns the computer to the executive (operating system) mode.

● **CALL:** The purpose of the CALL function is to enable the program to produce results that cannot be achieved by the BASIC language itself. The use of the CALL or USER statements allows the programmer to call upon a "machine language" subroutine. Most versions of BASIC require the programmer to reference the user-written code by addressing the first line of the

12 CALL

subroutine by its actual absolute location in the computer's memory. In certain versions of BASIC, the CALL statement can also be used to call a routine.

Other versions of BASIC use different keywords to accomplish the same or similar functions. These keywords are USR and SYS. The principle of operation is the same: there is a machine language program located somewhere in memory that the BASIC program is directed to during execution. After the CALL, the computer is usually returned to the statement following the CALL statement in the BASIC program.

EXAMPLE:

MACHINE LANGUAGE

10	CALL 936 (where 936 is the absolute location in memory of the routine, 936 is in decimal notation.)
20	CALL C9A (Where C9A is the absolute location in memory of the routine, C9A is in hexadecimal notation.)
30	CALL "PLOT" (Where "PLOT" is the routine.)

Using the CALL in conjunction with name subroutines, we can usually place variables after the routine name, separated by commas. These variables have assigned values which can be passed on to the routine as data.

EXAMPLE:

| 10 | CALL "PLOT", A,B,C |
| 20 | CALL "CONTROL",K,J,L |

Typical examples of the uses of the called machine language subroutines are control of floppy discs, tape drives, plotters, and externally controlled relays, switches, and other electronic equipment.

PROGRAMMING EXAMPLE:

10	REM THIS PROGRAM DEMONSTRATES THE
20	REM CALL OR USER FUNCTION.
30	CALL 936
40	LET N = 14
50	LET J = N*N
60	LET K = 18
70	CALL 1404

```
80     LET K = K - 1
90     IF K > = 10 THEN 70
100    END
```

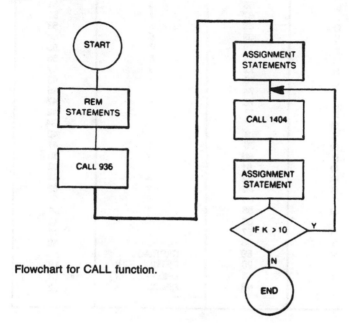

Flowchart for CALL function.

● **CAT:** The CATALOG or CAT command allows the user to view the list of names of all programs previously saved by the user.

Other computers use the commands FILES or DIR to obtain a list of previously saved programs. All these commands usually only apply to systems equipped with some form of disk storage, and not to tape-only systems.

● **CATALOG:** See *CAT*.

● **CHANGE:** When a computer stores the characters of a string, it does not store the characters directly, but as an encoded sequence of numbers.

Several different numerical coding schemes can be used, but the most common is the 7-bit ASCII code. The following table shows the ASCII (American Standard Code for Information Interchange) coding.

The computer automatically carries out the conversion from characters to numbers and the reverse. The operation is generally

CHARACTER	CODE	CHARACTER	CODE
A	65	2	50
B	66	3	51
C	67	4	52
D	68	5	53
E	69	6	54
F	70	7	55
G	71	8	56
H	72	9	57
I	73	+	43
J	74	–	45
K	75	/	47
L	76	*	42
M	77	↑	94
N	78	(	40
O	79	)	41
P	80	<	60
Q	81	>	62
R	82	=	61
S	83	?	63
T	84	$	36
U	85	"	34
V	86	,	44
W	87	.	46
X	88	;	59
Y	89	CARRIAGE	
Z	90	RETURN (CR)	13
0	48	LINE FEED (LF)	10
1	49	SPACE	32

transparent; that is, the user is not usually even aware of the fact that the computer is encoding the characters.

Sometimes it is necessary to use the numeric equivalent of the character in a string. This has the advantage of allowing the user to manipulate each character individually. This conversion is carried out by the CHANGE statement.

The CHANGE statement may be written in two different ways.

METHOD 1:

The keyword CHANGE, is followed by a string variable, the keyword TO, and a numeric list. The items in this statement must be kept in that order.

This statement causes each character in the string to be converted to its numerical equivalent and stored in a numeric list.

The first element in the numeric list (that is the element with a subscript of zero) will indicate the number of encoded characters contained in the list.

EXAMPLE:

```
10    LET J$ = "JANE"
20    . . . . . . . . . .
30    CHANGE J$ TO K
```

In the previous example the elements of K will be the following.

K(0) = 4
K(1) = 74
K(2) = 65
K(3) = 78
K(4) = 69

METHOD 2:

The string variable and the numeric list may be interchanged.

```
10    LET J(0) = 3
20    LET J(1) = 75
30    LET J(2) = 69
40    LET J(3) = 78
50    CHANGE J TO K$
```

In the example just shown, K$ will be assigned the string KEN.

PROGRAMMING EXAMPLE:

```
10    REM THIS PROGRAM DEMONSTRATES
20    REM THE CHANGE STATEMENT
30    PRINT "INPUT A WORD"
40    INPUT J$
50    CHANGE J$ TO K
60    FOR I = 0 TO LEN(J$)
70    PRINT K(I),
80    NEXT I
90    PRINT
100   PRINT "WE WILL NOW CHANGE NUMBERS TO A
      STRING"
110   PRINT "HOW MANY NUMBERS"
120   INPUT L
130   LET X(0) = L
140   FOR M = 1 TO L
150   PRINT "INPUT A NUMBER"
160   INPUT L
```

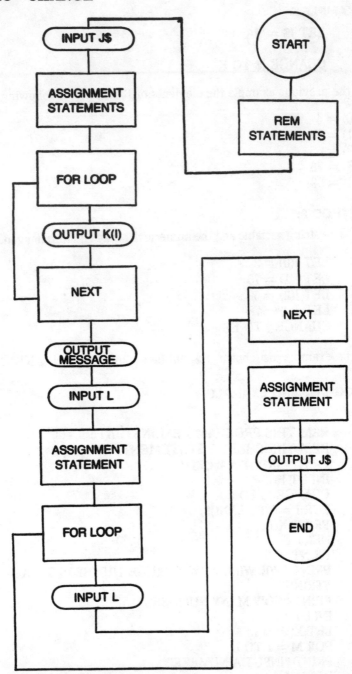

Flowchart for CHANGE statement.

```
170     LET X(M) = L
180     NEXT M
190     CHANGE X TO J$
200     PRINT J$
210     END
```

RUN

```
INPUT A WORD
?JAYN
4   74   65   89   78
WE WILL NOW CHANGE NUMBERS TO A STRING
HOW MANY NUMBERS
?3
INPUT A NUMBER
?75
INPUT A NUMBER
?69
INPUT A NUMBER
?78
KEN
```

END

Most microcomputers do not have the CHANGE function. If yours doesn't, you can use the ASC or CHR$ functions to get the same results.

For example, if your computer doesn't have the CHANGE function, and you want to change the string "JANE" to its ASCII equivalent, use the following program:

EXAMPLE:
```
10     LET J$ = "JANE"
20     LET K(0) = LEN(J$)
30     FOR I = 1 TO K(0)
40     LET D$ = MID$(J$,I,1)
50     LET K(I) = ASC(D$)
60     NEXT I
```

In this example, the FOR-NEXT loop selects the characters in J$ one at a time and stores the character in D$, in line 40. Line 50 converts the letter to its ASCII equivalent and stores it in the array variable K.

This program gives the same result as the first example program in METHOD 1.

For converting the other way, from an array of values to the string, use the following program:

EXAMPLE:

```
10    LET J(0) = 3
20    LET J(1) = 75
30    LET J(2) = 69
40    LET J(3) = 78
50    LET K$ = " "
60    FOR I = 1 TO J(0)
70    LET K$ = K$ + CHR$(J(I))
80    NEXT I
90    PRINT K$
```

READY

RUN

KEN

READY

This program gives the same result as the program shown in METHOD 2. To understand these programs a little better, see the functions *CHR$, MID, and LEN.*

● **CHR$:** The library function CHR$ is the opposite of the library function ASC. The CHR$ function converts an ASCII code into a character. Obviously the argument must be a recognized ASCII integer quantity. All noninteger values will be truncated.

EXAMPLE:

```
10    LET Z$ = CHR$(X)
20    LET K$ = CHR$(65)
30    LET H$ = CHR$(74)
40    LET K$ = CHR$(75)
```

PROGRAMMING EXAMPLE:

```
10    REM THIS PROGRAM DEMONSTRATES
20    REM THE CHR$ FUNCTION
```

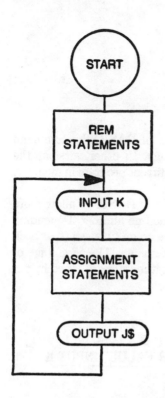

Flowchart for CHR$ function.

```
30    PRINT "INPUT A NUMBER"
40    INPUT K
45    IF K = 0 END
50    LET J$ = CHR$(K)
60    PRINT J$
70    GOTO 30
80    END

RUN

INPUT A NUMBER
?80
P
INPUT A NUMBER
?63
?
INPUT A NUMBER
?50
2
```

INPUT A NUMBER
?0
J

END

    ● **CLEAR:** In some versions of BASIC the command CLEAR zeroes all variables and strings. In other versions the CLEAR command clears or erases the current program in memory.

    ● **Colon(:):** The colon is used in BASIC to allow more than one statement to be included in one line number. Depending on the version of BASIC used either the colon (:), slash (/) or back slash (\) is used between different statements. The advantage of using multiple statements per line is that memory is saved by not having to specify as many line numbers.

EXAMPLE:
```
10    LET K =J/LET H = Z*2/LET P = 3.1415
20    PRINT:PRINT:PRINT "ENTER VALUE":INPUT K
```

The above may also be written as:
```
10    LET K = J: LET H = Z*2: LET P = 3.1415
```
or
```
20    PRINT\PRINT\PRINT "ENTER VALUE"\INPUT K
```

Depending on the version of BASIC caution must be exercised with conditional statements. Some versions fall through to the next statement in a multi-statement line, while others fall through to the next line number.

EXAMPLE:
```
10    IF X = Y THEN PRINT Y : GOTO 100
20    PRINT X
```

If the condition X = Y is true Y should be printed and the execution transferred to line 100. If the condition is not met, transfer should be given to line 100.

If the version of BASIC used had "fall through" to the next line, the true condition would work as just shown, but in the false condition transfer would go to line 20, not line 100. This occurs because after the conditional test is made and is found false, transfer goes to the next line, not to the next statement.

Also depending on the version being used, more than one line of code may be written under one line number. (Usually a fixed maximum of characters is set, typically around 255 for the number of characters in a multi-statement.)

EXAMPLE:

```
10   LET K = J: FOR I = 1 TO 20: PRINT I:
     PRINT: PRINT K*I: NEXT I
20   PRINT: PRINT "LOOP FINISHED": END
```

● **Concatenation:** Concatenation is the process of adding two or more strings together, such as "HELLO" and "JANE", to form one string, "HELLO JANE". In concatenation we use the + (plus) symbol and form an assignment statement using strings and/or string variables.

EXAMPLE:

```
10   LET K$ = J$ + L$
20   LET S$ = "MICE" + " " + "ARE" + " " + "NICE"
30   LET Z$ = "VALVE" + L$
40   LET H$ = Q$ + "ATOMS"
50   LET P$ = B$ + "ARE" + C$
```

Note: If spaces are required, they must either be part of the string or variable, or be concatenated separately, as line 20 of the previous example.

PROGRAMMING EXAMPLE:

```
10    REM THIS PROGRAM DEMONSTRATES
20    REM THE CONCATENATION FUNCTION
30    PRINT "ENTER ANY THREE WORDS"
40    INPUT J$,K$,L$
50    LET A$ = " "
60    LET B$ = J$ + A$ + K$ + A$ + L$
70    PRINT B$
80    IF B$ = "STOP NOW OK" THEN 100
90    GOTO 30
100   END
```

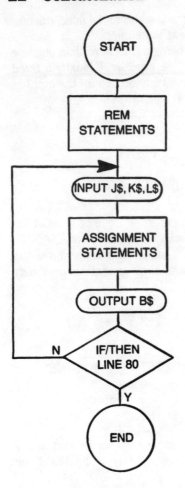

Flowchart for concatenation example.

```
RUN
ENTER ANY THREE WORDS
?MICE,ARE,NICE
MICE ARE NICE
ENTER ANY THREE WORDS
?THIS,IS,BASIC
THIS IS BASIC
ENTER ANY THREE WORDS
?STOP,NOW,OK
STOP NOW OK

END
```

● **Conditional Branching:** The IF-THEN statement is the basis of the conditional branching operation in BASIC. This statement consists of the key words IF and THEN, separated by a relation, and followed by the number of the line to be branched to. **Note:** In some versions of BASIC it is allowable to place an ASSIGNMENT or other statement after the THEN required.

EXAMPLE:

```
10     IF J = K THEN 100
20     IF X < > 10 THEN 120
30     IF J1 < 2 THEN 100
40     IF Q > 37 THEN 150
50     IF H > = 86 THEN 200
60     IF A < = 10 THEN 80
```

If the condition is satisfied, the branch will occur; otherwise, the next line will be executed.

For an IF-THEN statement that transfers control to another line, some versions of BASIC allow the use of the word GOTO instead of THEN.

EXAMPLE:

```
10     IF J = K GOTO 100
```

Conditional branching is used with strings as well as with numerics. In the case of a string as opposed to a string variable (i.e., A$), the string must be enclosed in quotation marks.

EXAMPLE:

```
10     IF K$ = "KEN" THEN 100
20     IF K$ = J$ THEN 500
```

PRGRAMMING EXAMPLE:

```
10     REM THIS PROGRAM DEMONSTRATES
20     REM THE IF-THEN STATEMENT
30     INPUT J
40     IF J = 0 THEN 70
50     PRINT "J IS NON-ZERO"
60     GOTO 30
70     PRINT "J IS ZERO"
80     GOTO 30
90     END
```

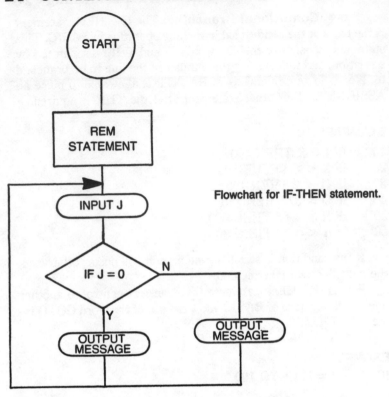

Flowchart for IF-THEN statement.

● **CONTINUE:** The CONTINUE command (CON or CONT in some versions of BASIC) restarts program execution after a CONTROL-C, CON, or CONT is entered.

● **Control Characters:** Control characters are generated by holding down the CTRL key while typing the specified letter. Generally the control character is not printed.

The following is a list of control characters. Remember to hold down the CTRL key while typing the letter specified!

```
C . . . . . Halts a program
G . . . . . Sounds bell
H . . . . . Backspaces cursor
J . . . . . Issues line feed
V . . . . . Forward spaces cursor
X . . . . . Deletes current line
```

Some microcomputers do not have control keys as such, but

instead come with, or can be programmed for, keys that can "act" as control keys. For example, if you are using a microcomputer to communicate with another computer, the communications program you use may define a certain key as the "control" key. To transmit a control character, you would hold down this key and the other designated key.

Another example is a word processing program requiring control functions. In this case, a specific key is designated as the control key—for example the "@" key. A sticker may be provided for the key to aid in recalling its location. Then all you do when you see the direction to press CONTROL-C is to press the "@" key, and, while still holding it down, press the "C" key. Both are then usually released, and the function requiring the CONTROL-C is invoked.

● **COPY:** Different versions of BASIC have different methods of controlling peripheral devices. The COPY command is usually used with a computer having both a video terminal (CRT) and a printer.

After typing in the keyword or command COPY, the computer will utilize the printer to make a "hard copy" of what is presently on the CRT screen.

Microcomputers have many variations of this command. In most, the purpose is the same: to direct the output of the computer to the printer and/or the screen. Some of these commands can be used inside a BASIC program; others must be used only from DOS (disk operating system). The forms of the commands differ widely and include ECHO, ROUTE, OPEN and DEVICE.

To use such a command, first decide what you want to have printed and when. Then see your programming reference manual to obtain the details of the specific form of the command required by your computer. Remember that not all computers will have this type of command, and don't forget about the LPRINT and LLIST statements and their relative, OPEN.

● **COS:** The library function COS returns the cosine of the argument in parentheses. The argument is generally interpreted as being in radians.

EXAMPLE:

```
10    PRINT COS(Y)
20    K = COS(J)
```

PROGRAMMING EXAMPLE:

```
10    REM THIS PROGRAM DEMONSTRATES
20    REM THE COS FUNCTION
30    PRINT "INPUT A NUMBER"
40    INPUT J
50    IF J = 0 THEN 80
60    PRINT COS(J)
70    GOTO 30
80    END
```

RUN

INPUT A NUMBER
?3.14159
− 1
INPUT A NUMBER
?1.2

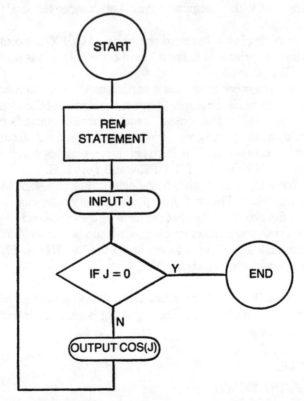

Flowchart for COS function.

0.36235
INPUT A NUMBER
?6.28319
1
INPUT A NUMBER
?0

END

● **DEF FN:** When a program section is used as a function, and is used quite often during the main program, the programmer can use the DEF FN statement.

DEF FN allows the user to write a function such as A = (A − 3)/A and use it repeatedly throughout the program by calling the function.

The DEF FN statement consists of the keyword DEF and the function definition. The function definition is the function name followed by an equal sign, followed by the appropriate variable, constant, or formula. Both numeric and string functions can be defined by the DEF FN statement. If the function requires arguments then they must appear directly after the function name, enclosed in parentheses and separated by commas.

If the function is numeric, the function name must consist of three letters, the first two being FN. Thus any given program may have 26 different numeric functions, ranging from FNA to FNZ. You may also have 26 different string functions labeled FNA$ to FNZ$. Numeric and string functions having the same first three letters, such as FNJ and FNJ$, are considered to be different functions. Thus any program may contain 52 functions. As can be seen, the string function name must end in a dollar sign.

EXAMPLE:

```
10    DEF FNJ(K,L) = (K − 2)/(L − 3)
20    DEF FNK$ = "EMPLOYEE STATUS"
30    DEF FNZ(X,Y) = (X − Y) − (Y − X)
```

A DEF FN statement may appear anywhere within the BASIC program. It is, however, considered good practice to group all the DEF FN statements together and place them near the beginning or end of the program.

It should be obvious that the DEF FN statement only defines a function but does **not** evaluate it.

PROGRAMMING EXAMPLE:

```
10    REM THIS PROGRAM DEMONSTRATES
20    REM THE DEF STATEMENT
30    DEF FNA(X) = LOG(X)/X
40    DEF FNB(X) = SIN(X)/K
50    DEF FNC(X) = COS(X)/L
60    PRINT "INPUT A NUMBER"
70    INPUT J
80    LET J = ABS(J)
90    LET K = 10
100   LET L = 20
110   LET M = FNA(J)
120   LET N = FNB(J)
130   LET P = FNC(J)
140   PRINT M,N,P
150   END
```

RUN

INPUT A NUMBER

?8
0.25993   0.09894   -0.00728

END

In this example, you can see another property of the DEF FN statement. Any variables (K, L) not included in parentheses (nondefined arguments) in the DEF FN statement name will be used as having the most recent values assigned to them.

● **DET:** Once we determine the inverse of a square matrix we may further determine its determinant by using the library function DET. The DET function returns a single numeric value and requires no argument. One obvious use of the DET statement is to determine if a given matrix does have an inverse. If the inverse does not exist, the determinant will be zero.

Note: The DET library function may only be referenced after a MAT INV statement. If the DET function returns a zero for a given matrix, the inverse determined by the preceding MAT INV statement will not be meaningful.

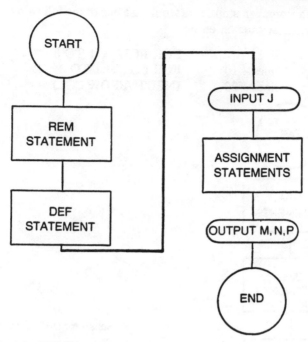

Flowchart for DEF FN statement.

Most versions of microcomputer BASIC do not have the matrix-associated functions built in. If you have to find the determinant of a (square) matrix, here's a small example of a 3-×-3 matrix:

$$
\begin{array}{ccc}
A(1,1) & A(1,2) & A(1,3) \\
A(2,1) & A(2,2) & A(2,3) \\
A(3,1) & A(3,2) & A(3,3)
\end{array}
$$

The equation for the determinant D of the 3-×-3 matrix is:

$$
\begin{aligned}
D = {} & A(1,1)A(2,2)A(3,3) + A(1,2)A(2,3)A(3,1) \\
& + A(1,3)A(2,1)A(3,1) - A(1,1)A(2,3)A(3,2) \\
& - A(1,2)A(2,1)A(3,3) - A(1,3)A(2,2)A(3,1)
\end{aligned}
$$

The program for finding the determinant of the matrix would then follow these steps:

1. Place the values for each element of the matrix into the array A.

2. Calculate the value of the determinant and place the value in D.

30 DET

To accomplish step 1, we would use one of the following kinds of program segments, either:

line#	FOR ROW = 1 TO 3
line# + 10	FOR COL = 1 TO 3
line# + 20	INPUT A(ROW,COL)

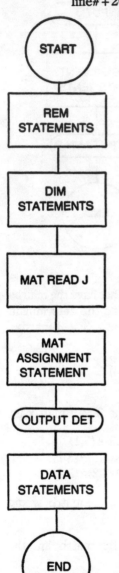

Flowchart for DET function.

line#+30   NEXT ROW
line#+40   NEXT COL
etc . . .

or we could substitute: line#+20 READ A(ROW,COL) for the same line shown, if the values were held in DATA statements.

Once the values of the elements of the matrix have been placed in the array A, we could then transfer the computer to the following statement to find the value of the determinant and place its value into the variable D:

$$\text{line\#}+50 \quad D = A(1,1)*A(2,2)*A(3,3) + A(1,2)*A(2,3)*A(3,1)$$
$$+ A(1,3)*A(2,1)*A(3,2) - A(1,1)*A(2,3)*A(3,2)$$
$$- A(1,2)*A(2,1)*A(3,3) - A(1,3)*A(2,2)*A(3,1)$$

The length of the line may be too long for many computers, so if you need to break it up, just use, say, the first three terms of the calculation in the line, then follow it with a line like this:

$$\text{line\#}+60 \quad D = D - A(1,1)*A(2,3)*A(3,2) - \ldots$$

This, and the other matrix, or MAT, functions are good examples of the needs of modern microcomputer programmers. If your computer doesn't have a particular function that you need, look for a way to create that function. Get out your old math book; find a friend knowledgeable enough to help, and write a short program to give the desired function. You'll get the job done, and who knows—have some fun in the process!

EXAMPLE:

```
10    MAT J = INV(K)
20    PRINT DET
```

PROGRAMMING EXAMPLE:

```
10    REM THIS PROGRAM DEMONSTRATES
20    REM THE DET FUNCTION
30    DIM J(5,5),K(5,5),L(5,5)
40    MAT READ J
50    MAT K = INV(J)
60    PRINT DET
70    DATA 6,8,9,4,1,2,4,6,2,4,8,9,2,1,3
80    DATA 7,3,2,1,4,6,5,3,1,4
90    END
```

● **DIM:** Most BASIC versions require a DIM statement to be placed before an array (subscripted variable) is used. If the array does not have more than 10 or 11 elements, most versions of BASIC will automatically allow their use by "default" (see the next paragraph). For arrays having more than 10 elements, a DIM statement is usually required before the first use of the variable. If you try to use the DIM statement after the array's first use, you will usually get an error message. Also, most versions of BASIC do not allow more than one DIM statement for a particular variable. If you try to DIMension a variable a second time, the computer will probably give you an error message.

Some versions of BASIC assign 121 elements (11 columns, 11 rows to every table and 11 elements to every list. Thus each subscript can generally range from 0 to 10 (occasionally 1 to 11). In versions of BASIC which do not automatically assign elements to lists and tables, or if you desire more than 11 elements to a list or 11 rows by 11 columns to a table, you must use the DIMension (DIM) statement.

The DIM statement consists of the keyword DIM followed by various array names, separated by commas. Each and every array name must be followed by at least one number (for lists) or two numbers separated by a comma for tables. In either case, the numeric values are placed in parentheses directly following the array name.

EXAMPLE:

```
10    DIM J(19), K(28), L(4), M(8,10)
20    DIM A(10,20), B(250), X(65), J$(35)
30    DIM F(9), K$(14,14), J$(9,10)
```

A DIM statement can occur anywhere in a BASIC program, but it is considered good practice to place all DIM statements at the very beginning.

PROGRAMMING EXAMPLE:

```
10    REM THIS PROGRAM DEMONSTRATES THE
20    REM DIM STATEMENT
30    DIM A$(20),B$(3),C(60)
40    FOR I = 1 TO 60
50    LET C(I) = I
60    NEXT I
70    END
```

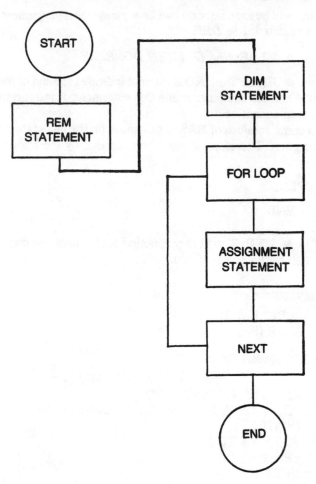

Flowchart for DIM statement.

- **DIMENSION:** See *DIM*.

- **DO END:** See *IF-THEN DO, ELSE*

- **Dummy Arguments:** Whenever a certain function requires an argument in advance, such as the DEF statement, the actual value of the argument is not required. What is required is the number and type of arguments being used. An argument that only expresses location, type, and use is called a *dummy argument*. A dummy argument "tells" the function in advance that a numeric or string will be used later on and how many "real" arguments are to be evaluated. See *DEF*.

● **ELSE:** See *IF-THEN DO, ELSE*

● **END:** The END statement indicates the end of the program. When the computer reads this statement, it interprets it to mean stop execution.

In some versions of BASIC this must be the last statement in the program. Therefore, it must be preceded by the highest line number.

EXAMPLE:

```
999    END
```

● **EXP:** The library function EXP raises the constant *e* (2.71828) to the power X (e^x).

EXAMPLES:

```
10     PRINT EXP(J)
20     Z = EXP(Q)
```

PROGRAMMING EXAMPLE:

```
10     REM THIS PROGRAM DEMONSTRATES
20     REM THE EXP FUNCTION
30     PRINT "INPUT A NUMBER FROM 1 TO 10"
40     INPUT J
50     FOR I = 1 TO J
60     PRINT EXP(I)
70     NEXT I
80     END
```

RUN

```
INPUT A NUMBER FROM 1 TO 10
?6
2.71828
7.38906
20.0855
54.5981
148.413
403.429
END
```

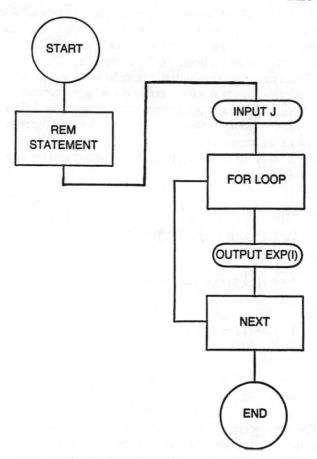

Flowchart for EXP function.

● **File:** A *file* consists of a group of records, where each record may be considered to be a group of variables.

To use a filing cabinet for comparison, a variable is a line of printing, a number, or a slip. A record is a file folder. The whole drawer, cabinet, or aisle of cabinets, is the file.

Files usually contain related data, but this is the programmer's decision.

As every version of BASIC has its own way of defining files and file handling, it is always best to consult the user's manual for the computer being used. See also *Sequential Data Files* and *Random Data Files*.

● **FN:** To reference a function predefined by a DEF statement, a typical assignment statement is written with the function name acting as though it were a library function, with the function name followed in parentheses by an argument.

When a function is evaluated, the values of the arguments are specified by the function referenced and not by the function definition. For this reason any arguments appearing with a DEF statement are called *dummy arguments*. The arguments in the reference need not be the same as those appearing in the definition, but they must be of the same type (i.e., numeric or string) and number. See *Dummy Arguments*.

EXAMPLE:

```
10    DEF FNK(J) = (J − 3)/J
20    ..........
30    ..........
40    LET H = FNK(Z) −100
50    ..........
60    ..........
70    IF FNK(P) = 110 THEN 100
80    PRINT FNK(A)
90    STOP
100   PRINT "SOLUTION IS";P
110   END
```

The arguments in the reference must have a one-to-one correspondence with the dummy arguments when two or more arguments are used. The correspondence is not by name, but by type and number of arguments.

Dummy arguments must be nonsubscripted variables, but the arguments present in the function reference may be written as constants, subscripted variables, formulas, or even other references.

PROGRAMMING EXAMPLE:

```
10    REM THIS PROGRAM DEMONSTRATES
20    REM THE FN STATEMENT
30    DEF FNA(X) = LOG(X)*2
40    FOR I = 1 TO 10
50    PRINT FNA(I)
60    NEXT I
70    END
```

RUN

0
1.38628
2.19722
2.77258
3.21886
3.58352
3.89182
4.15888
4.39444
4.60516

END

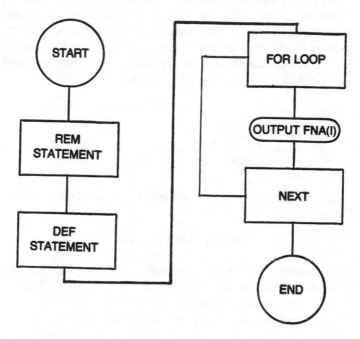

Flowchart for FN statement.

● **FOR-TO:** In BASIC, if we know how many times a loop should be performed we use the FOR-TO statement, which specifies how many times the loop is to be executed. Directly following the keyword FOR is the running variable, which must be a non-subscripted numeric variable, whose value changes each time the loop is executed. The number of times the loop is executed is specified by the initial and final values of the running variable.

EXAMPLE:

```
10      FOR J = 1 TO 50
20      FOR K = 10 TO 100
30      FOR L = 7 TO 10
```

If we set up a FOR-TO statement such as,

$$FOR\ I = 1\ TO\ 10$$

I is initially set to 1. I is then incremented by 1 each time the loop is repeated, until I has reached the final value of 10.

The running variable will always be incremented by 1 unless a contrary statement is included. The STEP statement changes the value by which I changes. Using the STEP statement, we may increment or decrement the running variable. In most versions of BASIC we can also use variables or formulas for the initial and final values of the running variable and the step size.

EXAMPLE:

```
10      FOR J = K TO X STEP Z
20      FOR K = 1 TO Q STEP -Z
30      FOR J = K/L TO M+ L STEP K-1
```

Some versions of BASIC allow the interchange of the keywords STEP and BY. Thus we can have:

$$FOR\ K = J\ TO\ M\ BY\ L$$

To close the FOR-TO loop we use the keyword NEXT. All FOR-TO loops must end in a NEXT statement. The NEXT statement consists of a statement number (line number) and the keyword NEXT, followed by the running variable name. Of course the running variable must be the running variable used in the corresponding FOR-TO statement.

EXAMPLE:

```
10      FOR K = J TO M
20      ..........
30      ..........
```

```
40      ..........
50      ..........
60      NEXT K
```

The following rules always apply in the FOR-TO-STEP loop:

1) The running variable may appear in a statement within the loop, but its value must not and can not be changed or altered.
2) If the final and initial values of the running variable are equal and the step size is nonzero, the loop will be executed once.
3) The loop will not be executed under the following conditions:
   A) The final and initial running variable values are equal, and the step size is zero.
   B) The final value is less than the initial value, and the step size is positive.
   C) The final value is greater than the initial value, and the step size is negative.
4) Control can be transferred out of a loop but not into one.

PROGRAMMING EXAMPLE:

```
10      REM THIS PROGRAM DEMONSTRATES
20      REM THE FOR-TO STATEMENT
30      FOR I = 1 TO 10
40      PRINT I*10
50      NEXT I
60      END
```

RUN

```
10
20
30
40
50
60
70
80
90
100
END
```

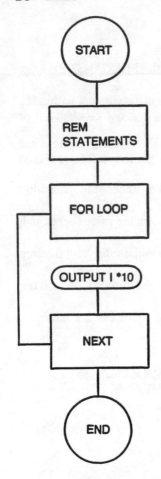

Flowchart for FOR-TO statement.

● **FRE:** The FRE statement requires either a zero as an argument, which returns the number of memory bytes currently unused by BASIC not including strings,

EXAMPLE:

10   PRINT FRE(0)

or A\$ as an argument, which returns the number of unused memory bytes including strings.

Other variations of the FRE statement are found in different implementations of BASIC. In some, FRE(A\$) returns only the amount of space available for string storage.

Another keyword sometimes used is MEM. PRINT MEM, in those cases, returns the space available, not including space for string storage.

EXAMPLE:

10   PRINT FRE(A$)

● **GOSUB:** A subroutine is referenced by the keyword GOSUB followed by the line number of the first statement in the subroutine structure. When the computer executes this instruction, control is transferred to the line indicated by the GOSUB statement, but the computer "remembers" the line in the program where the subroutine call was generated. On encountering a RETURN statement, the computer returns control to the statement following the one that was kept in memory. That is, control is transferred to the statement immediately following the subroutine call.

EXAMPLE:

```
10      LET J = 25
20      LET K = 2
30      GOSUB 60
40      PRINT L
50      ..........
60      LET L = J/K
70      RETURN
```

Note: Unless the statement prior to the first statement of the subroutine is a branch or a STOP statement, the subroutine will be executed as part of the main program.

A program may contain more than one reference to the same subroutine procedure. Control will always be returned to the statement following the point of call.

EXAMPLE:

```
10      LET A = 10
20      LET B = 2
30      GOSUB 100
40      PRINT C
50      GOSUB 100
60      PRINT C-2
70      ..........
```

80	....
90	....
100	LET C = A/B
110	RETURN

A subroutine itself may call a subroutine. This is called *nesting* (see *Nested Loops*). The number of levels in the nest is determined by the version of BASIC used. The following rule always applies with nested subroutines: if Subroutine X calls Subroutine Z, then Subroutine Z must not call Subroutine X.

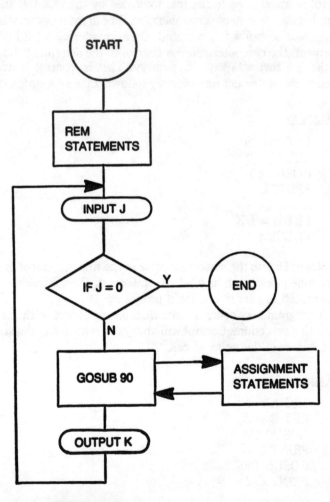

Flowchart for GOSUB statement.

PROGRAMMING EXAMPLE:

```
10      REM THIS PROGRAM DEMONSTRATES
20      REM THE GOSUB STATEMENT
30      PRINT "ENTER A NUMBER"
40      INPUT J
50      IF J = 0 THEN 110
60      GOSUB 90
70      PRINT K
80      GOTO 30
90      LET K = (J*2)/3
100     RETURN
110     END
```

RUN

```
ENTER A NUMBER
?5
3.33333
ENTER A NUMBER
?1256
837.333
ENTER A NUMBER
?31.3
20.8666
ENTER A NUMBER
?0

END
```

● **GOTO:** In a BASIC program the flow of execution is from the smallest line number to the largest line number. If an *unconditional* jump is required—a jump that requires no logic to see if it is to be performed or not—a GOTO statement is used. The GOTO statement or unconditional jump is usually referred to as an *unconditional branch statement.* The GOTO statement can transfer control to any other statement with the program. Once the branch is completed, execution flow continues from the smallest to the largest line number.

EXAMPLE:

```
10      GOTO 100
20      GOTO 1090
```

44 GOTO

It should be noted that depending on the version of BASIC used GOTO may be one word, two words, or either.

PROGRAMMING EXAMPLE:

```
10      REM THIS PROGRAM DEMONSTRATES CONDI-
        TIONAL
20      REM BRANCHING OUT OF A GOTO LOOP
30      REM THIS PROGRAM COMPUTES THE AVERAGE
40      REM OF N NUMBERS
50      REM TO EXIT THE LOOP TYPE A 0
60      LET K = 0
70      LET N = 0
80      INPUT J
90      IF J = 0 THEN 130
100     LET K = K + J
```

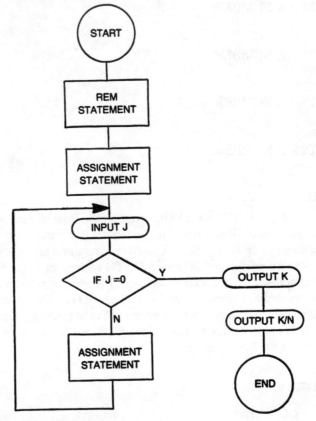

Flowchart for GOTO Loop.

```
110     LET N = N + 1
120     GOTO 80
130     PRINT "SUM = ";K
140     PRINT "AVERAGE = ";K/N
150     END
```

● **Graphical Output:** The numeric lists or tables produced by computer programs are often plotted by hand on graph paper, but it is very useful if the computer can produce graphical output without special equipment. A CRT video terminal is not usually a good choice because the resolution of graph depends upon the number of horizontal and vertical positions available. Although both the CRT and typical printers have the same number of horizontal positions, the printer can produce literally infinite vertical positions, if we view the length as vertical. Alternatively, the paper's width could be viewed as vertical, and thus we can have an extended horizontal graph.

The easiest method for producing a graph is to use a FOR-TO loop which has a PRINT statement containing the TAB function within the structure.

The following are typical routines that may be used in the production of graphs.

X AXIS (axis across the width of the paper)
```
10      FOR J = 0 TO 71
20      PRINT TAB(J);".";
30      NEXT J
```

Y AXIS (along the length of the paper)
Since we are plotting the graph along the length of the paper, we must plot the Y axis (length axis) at the same time.

```
10      FOR B = Y TO Z
20      ..........
30      ..........
40      PRINT ".";  TAB(A);"*"
50      ..........
60      ..........
70      NEXT B
```

Line 40 prints both the Y axis and also the graph, in this case composed of asterisks (*). Lines 20, 30, 50, and 60 generate the values for A. Obviously A is being plotted against B; as each cycle

of the loop moves along the Y axis, the TAB function places the
* in the proper position as determined by the formula generating
the value of A.

If it is desirable to produce graphs on the CRT, most microcomputer BASIC languages allow for at least low- or medium-resolution
graphics. These are usually sufficient to provide good bar graphs
on the screen, sometimes even in color.

High-resolution graphics are complicated, and differ from one
computer to another, so we will not attempt an explanation here.

For producing low- or medium-resolution graphics on the CRT,
the approach just described would work all right. Similar dot or
asterisk positions would be visible on the screen as were printed
on paper. There are, however, often other ways available.

To try these on your computer, look in your reference manual
for the statements *Print@, SET, RESET, POKE, DRAW,* and
LINE. There are even more variations, with new ones appearing
all the time.

When you find yours, try one of the following routines (if the
statements are permitted in your version of BASIC). Several are
given so that if one is not recognized by your computer, perhaps
another will work.

EXAMPLE:

```
10   CLS
20   FOR J = 0 TO 40
30   PRINT TAB(J);".";
40   NEXT J
```

Observe the similarity between this routine and the X AXIS
routine. Many versions of BASIC differentiate between the printer
and the screen by using PRINT for screen output and LPRINT
for printer output.

The next routine uses the POKE statement. Be sure you have
looked at this definition closely, because it requires that you know
the location of your screen memory block for your computer. Once
you have found the screen memory, let's call this decimal number
SSSS. In place of the number NN, first try the ASCII code for an
asterisk, 42.

EXAMPLE:

```
10   CLS
20   FOR I = SSSS TO SSSS + 40
```

```
30  POKE I,NN
40  NEXT I
```

After this is working, try other codes in place of 42 for the value of NN, such as 36 for a dollar sign, or 65 for the letter A. If your version of BASIC includes graphics characters, try some of them. Often, the graphics codes are numbers above 128 and less than 256. If you try a number greater than 255 for NN, an error message will probably occur.

This routine draws a line of 40 characters across the screen. To vary the length of the line, change the 40 in line 20 to the desired length.

To draw a line vertically on the screen in the same way, use the width of your screen for the value of WW, and try this routine:

EXAMPLE:

```
10  CLS
20  FOR I = SSSS TO SSSS + 10*WW STEP WW
30  POKE I,NN
40  NEXT I
```

When this routine is run, a vertical line is drawn, placing 11 characters, one below the other. Use the value 42 for NN, the asterisk character, or another value between 32 and 255 for a different character.

● **Hierarchy:** When two or more operators are used in the same linear formula, questions in meaning may arise. Consider the case of 28*K—19*J. Does this correspond to the algebraic term (28K)—(19J) or to 28(K—19J)? Also consider K/J*4. Is this K/(4J) or 4(K/J)? These problems are taken care of by the following hierarchy of operations:

1) All exponentiation operations are performed first.
2) Multiplication and division are carried out after exponentiation. Multiplication and division have no hierarchy over each other; one will not necessarily preceed the other.
3) Addition and subtraction are always the last to be carried out. Here also no hierarchy exists between the two.

Within any given hierarchical group, the operations are carried out from left to right.

Parentheses change the order of normal hierarchical flow in a formula. See *Parentheses*.

Variation among versions of BASIC is present here, too, but most mathematicians use this listing of the standard order of the arithmetic operations:

Operation	Symbol	Example
Exponentiation	Up arrow	X ↟ Y
Negation	Minus sign	– N
Multiplication	Asterisk	A * B
Division	Slash	C / D
Addition	Plus sign	E + F
Subtraction	Minus sign	G – H

Don't be confused by the apparent double use of the minus sign. In the first case, negation, the sign is simply applied to make its argument, N, into a negative number. For subtraction two numbers, represented by G and H, are processed to find their difference.

Be on the alert for different symbols. Your BASIC may, for example, use the caret instead of the up arrow to indicate exponentiation.

In addition to the hierarchy for arithmetic operations just given, there are also hierarchies for logical operations (such as AND, OR, and NOT), and for relational operations (such as $=, >,$ and $< >$).

● **HOME:** The HOME command instructs the computer to return the display cursor to the "home" position, which is usually either the upper left or lower left corner of the CRT screen. Some versions of BASIC use a CALL or USER statement to achieve the same results.

Another commonly used keyword is CLS.

Some differences will be encountered when using these statements. HOME, for example usually only moves the cursor to the upper left of the screen, without disturbing the screen contents. Using CLS, on the other hand, usually clears the screen and moves the cursor to the upper left position.

When the BASIC allows the use of PRINT "HOME" and/or PRINT "CLR-HOME", the first is the equivalent of the HOME statement and the second, CLS. The "HOME" refers to pressing the HOME key, while "CLR-HOME" requires the SHIFT and HOME keys be pressed together.

- **IF-END:** See *Sequential Data Files Reading or Writing*.
- **IF-THEN:** See *Conditional Branching*.
- **IF-THEN DO, ELSE:** The IF-THEN DO, ELSE statement occurs in certain versions of BASIC and allows the user to write a complete procedure in the lines between the IF-THEN DO and the ELSE. Following the ELSE statement the user may also write a complete procedure. The line following the procedure after the ELSE and after the DO must contain only the keyword DOEND (DO END).

The format is therefore the following:

```
10      IF(EXPRESSION) THEN DO
20      ...........procedure.....................
30      .........................................
40      DO END
50      ELSE (EXPRESSION OR STATEMENT)
60      DO END
```

- **INPUT:** The input statement is used to enter numeric or string data into the computer during program execution. This statement consists of the keyword INPUT, followed by the list of variables separated by commas. Both numeric and string variables may be included in one INPUT statement.

EXAMPLE:

```
10      INPUT K,J
20      INPUT K$, J$, S$
30      INPUT K1$, J, S3$
```

During program execution, a question mark (?) is sent to the output device when an INPUT statement is encountered. The question mark is usually placed on a new line unless a PRINT statement previous to it included a semicolon as its last character.

An INPUT statement may also be combined with a PRINT statement as follows:

EXAMPLE:

INPUT "HOW OLD ARE YOU";J

In this case the computer will print the string HOW OLD ARE YOU on a new line, immediately follow it with a question mark,

50 INPUT

and wait for the input data.

In either case, when the INPUT statement is encountered and the question mark has been printed, the computer will suspend program execution until the data has been entered. After the data has been entered, the user must hit the return key to tell the computer that the data has been entered, and that it can continue execution.

The following rules must be adhered to when using the INPUT statement:

1) The data entered must correspond to the variables listed in the INPUT statement.

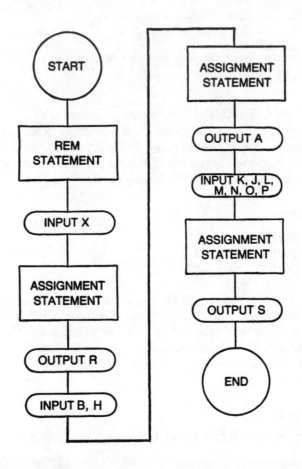

Flowchart for INPUT statement.

2) The data entered, if it is more than one item, must be separated by commas.

3) A string that contains a comma, begins with a blank space, or ends in a blank space, must be placed in quotation marks.

The INPUT statement is used for the conversation mode of BASIC and when large quantities of data are not required. If large volumes of data are required, the READ, DATA statements should be used.

PROGRAMMING EXAMPLE:

```
10    REM THIS PROGRAM DEMONSTRATES THE
20    REM INPUT STATEMENT
30    INPUT X
40    LET R = (X/3.14159)**.5
50    PRINT "RADIUS = ";R
60    INPUT B,H
70    LET A = (B*H)/2
80    PRINT "AREA = ";A
90    INPUT K,J,L,M,N,O,P
100   LET S = K + J + L + M + N + O + P
110   PRINT "SUM = ";S
120   END
```

● **INSTR:** This function searches for a second string within the first string. The keyword INSTR is followed in parentheses by a numeric formula, and the two string formulas.

To illustrate:

```
10    LET P = INSTR (X, Y$, Z$)
```

X is a numeric formula (constant or variable) truncated to an integer and indicates the starting position of the search. If X is not present, the first character of the string to be searched, is the starting position by default. Y is the string being sought for, and Z is the string being searched.

INSTR returns the position of the first character in the sub-STRING if found, 0 if not.

The value X, the starting position of the search, is optional. If the value is omitted, the string search begins at the leftmost character of the searched string, Z$. In the programming example given here, the value of X has been omitted.

52 INSTR

EXAMPLE:

```
10      LET P = INSTR(10,J$,K$)
20      LET P = INSTR(C,"A",J$)
30      LET P = INSTR("BYE","GOODBYE")
```

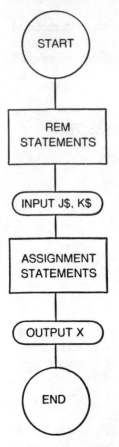

Flowchart for INSTR function.

PROGRAMMING EXAMPLE:

```
10      REM THIS PROGRAM DEMONSTRATES
20      REM THE INSTR FUNCTION
30      PRINT "ENTER TWO WORDS, THE FIRST MUST"
40      PRINT "BE CONTAINED IN THE SECOND"
50      INPUT J$,K$
60      LET X = INSTR(J$,K$)
70      PRINT X
80      END
```

RUN

ENTER TWO WORDS, THE FIRST MUST
BE CONTAINED IN THE SECOND
?BYE,GOODBYE
5

END

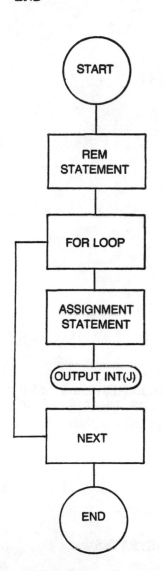

Flowchart for INT function.

● **INT:** The library function INT returns the largest integer less than or equal to the argument enclosed in parentheses.

EXAMPLE:

```
10    PRINT INT(Q)
20    Z = INT(X + Y)
```

PROGRAMMING EXAMPLE:

```
10    REM THIS PROGRAM DEMONSTRATES
20    REM THE INT FUNCTION
30    FOR I = 1 TO 10
40    LET J = I/3
50    PRINT INT(J)
60    NEXT I
70    END
```

RUN

```
0
0
1
1
1
2
2
2
3
3
```

END

● **LEFT$:** The library function LEFT$ returns the leftmost N characters of a string expression X$. Usually in BASIC, N must be greater than or equal to zero and less than 255.

EXAMPLE:

```
10    PRINT LEFT$(X$,N)
20    PRINT LEFT$(J$,10)
```

PROGRAMMING EXAMPLE:

```
10    REM THIS PROGRAM DEMONSTRATES
```

```
20    REM THE LEFT$ FUNCTION
30    INPUT J$
40    FOR N = 1 TO LEN(J$)
50    PRINT LEFT$(J$,N)
60    NEXT N
70    END
```

RUN

```
?A BASIC PROGRAM
A
A
A B
A BA
A BAS
A BASI
A BASIC
A BASIC
A BASIC P
```

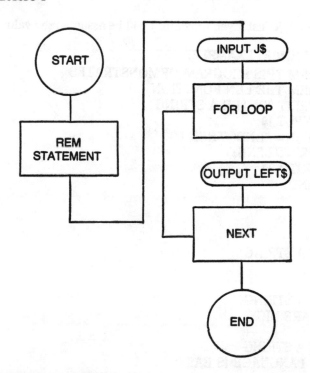

Flowchart for LEFT$ function.

A BASIC PR
A BASIC PRO
A BASIC PROG
A BASIC PROGR
A BASIC PROGRA
A BASIC PROGRAM

END

● **LEN:** The LEN library function computes the number of characters in a string. It is written as LEN followed by the string in parentheses. Some versions require the string to be also enclosed in quotation marks unless the variable is reference only.

EXAMPLE:

```
10    K = LEN("HOUSE")
20    H = LEN(A$)
30    J = LEN("JANE")
```

In the example just given (line 30), J will be assigned the value 4.

PROGRAMMING EXAMPLE:

```
10    REM THIS PROGRAM DEMONSTRATES
20    REM THE LEN FUNCTION
30    PRINT "ENTER A STRING"
40    INPUT J$
50    IF J$ = "END" THEN 80
60    PRINT LEN(J$)
70    GOTO 30
80    END
```

RUN

```
ENTER A STRING
? HELLO
5
ENTER A STRING
?MICE ARE NICE
13
ENTER A STRING
?BASIC LANGUAGE IS EASY
21
```

ENTER A STRING
?END

END

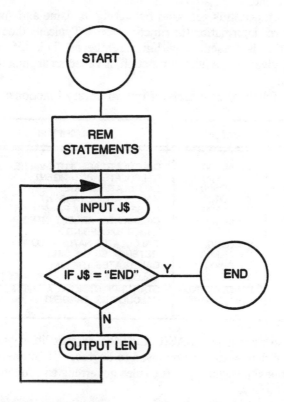

FLOWCHART for LEN function.

● **LENGTH:** LENGTH is generally a BASIC command, not a statement. It is used to ascertain the length of the current program residing in memory. When the user types in LENGTH during command mode, the total number of characters will be displayed.

● **LET:** See *Assignment.*

● **Library Functions:** The library functions, often called elementary or standard functions, provide a quick and easy method of evaluating mathematical operations and, in some versions of BASIC, logical operations.

The library functions are prewritten routines that are included as an integral part of the BASIC language. By using the library functions, the user can avoid writing an explicit routine to achieve the same end.

Each function is accessed by stating its name and supplying the required information the function needs. Typically the required information is presented within parentheses. This information, which is given to the library function, is called an argument of the function.

The following is a table of typical library functions:

FUNCTION	USAGE	DESCRIPTION
ABS	Y = ABS(X)	CALCULATE ABSOLUTE VALUE
ATN	Y = ATN(X)	CALCULATE ARCTANGENT
COS	Y = COS(X)	CALCULATE COSINE
COT	Y = COT(X)	CALCULATE COTANGENT
EXP	Y = EXP(X)	RAISE E TO THE X POWER
INT	Y = INT(X)	CALCULATE LARGEST INTEGER NOT EXCEEDING X
LOG	Y = LOG(X)	CALCULATES NATURAL LOG
SGN	Y = SGN(X)	DETERMINES THE SIGN
SIN	Y = SIN(X)	CALCULATES THE SINE
SQR	Y = SQR(X)	CALCULATES THE SQUARE ROOT
TAB	PRINT TAB(N)X	STARTS PRINTING AT A GIVEN COLUMN
TAN	Y = TAN(X)	CALCULATES TANGENT

In most versions of BASIC, the trigonometric library functions use the radian system as opposed to degrees. Of course, as with conventional mathematics, the rules governing trig functions and logs still apply.

● **Line Numbers:** Every BASIC program demands that each line of code be preceeded by a line number. Some versions of BASIC allow more than one statement per line and more than one line of code per line number.

It is a good idea to write the program starting at line 10 and incrementing by 10 for each line number to allow for inserts.

The BASIC language will automatically insert new lines of code according to their line numbers. If the line number used for the insert already exists, the old line will be replaced by the new.

Except for branching deliberately introduced by the programmer BASIC is always executed from smallest to largest line number.

● **LIST:** The LIST command displays the program,

starting from the smallest line number and ascending to the largest. The LIST command comes in a few different "varieties:"

LIST:	Lists the total program.
LIST X:	Lists line X if it exists.
LIST X-:	Lists all line numbers in a program with a line number equal to or greater than X.
LIST-X:	Lists all line numbers in a program equal to or less than X.
LIST X-Y:	Lists all line numbers in a program from X to Y.
LIST X,Y:	Same as LIST X-Y.

● **Lists and Tables:** When writing a complex or even a not-so-complex program, it is often convenient and useful to be able to refer to an entire collection of data at one time. A collection of data in BASIC is called an *array*. We can have a one-dimensional array, usually called a list, or we can have a two-dimensional array, the table. Most versions of BASIC allow us to refer to the elements of the lists and tables as if they were ordinary variables. This way of handling arrays simplifies array manipulation.

The elements of a list or array can usually be either numeric or string. **Note:** All the elements must be of the same type, either numeric or string but not both. Some versions of BASIC allow strings to be present in lists but not in tables.

Within one program each array must have a unique name, thus no two arrays can share the same letter or letter-dollar sign. If the array is numeric, it must be named by a simple letter; if it is a string array, it must be named by a letter followed by a dollar sign. Usually array names cannot be subscripted, i.e., letter-integer or letter-integer-dollar sign.

An ordinary variable and an array may share the same name. Unfortunately this becomes rather confusing and is thus not recommended. See *Subscript Variables*.

● **LOAD:** The LOAD command instructs the computer to take an already written program into its memory, usually from tape or disc. The LOAD command typically requires an argument, usually the name of the program desired.

EXAMPLES:

LOAD,MATH-TEST
LOAD,SPACE-WARS

● **LOC:** See *Random Data File Pointer Control.*

● **LOF:** See *Random Data File Pointer Control.*

● **LOG:** The library function LOG returns the natural (Base e) logarithm of the argument in parentheses.

EXAMPLE:

```
10    PRINT LOG(J)
20    Q = LOG(J/K)
```

PROGRAMMING EXAMPLE:

```
10    REM THIS PROGRAM DEMONSTRATES
20    REM THE LOG FUNCTION
30    PRINT "ENTER A BASE AND AN ARGUMENT
40    INPUT J,K
50    IF J = 0 OR K = 0 THEN 80
60    PRINT LOG(K)/LOG(J)
70    GOTO 30
80    END
```

RUN

```
ENTER A BASE AND AN ARGUMENT
?10,5
0.69897
ENTER A BASE AND AN ARGUMENT
?2,4
2
ENTER A BASE AND AN ARGUMENT
?1.34, 8.96
7.49231
ENTER A BASE AND AN ARGUMENT
?0,0
END
```

● **LONG:** In some versions of BASIC, double-precision mathematics and variables are allowed. To indicate that a variable

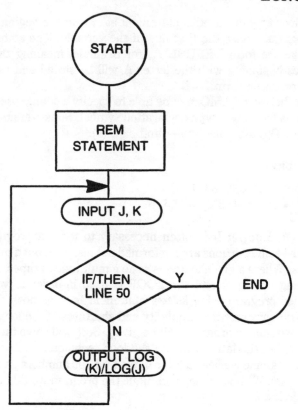

Flowchart for LOG function.

is a double-precision variable, the variable name is preceded by the keyword LONG on a line prior to the use of the variable in a function. Typically, double precision produces 12-digit variables. If a variable is indicated to be double precision, any operation on that variable will also produce a double-precision output. If an assignment is required, the variables on both sides of the equal sign must be indicated as being double precision.

EXAMPLE:

```
10    LONG J
20    LONG K
30    PRINT LOG(J)
40    LET K = SQR(J)
```

In other versions of BASIC, double-precision variables are initiated by a type declaration statement at or near the beginning of the program, before the first use of the variable. The statement may take the form DEFDBL A, for example, meaning that all variables beginning with the letter A will be stored and used in double-precision form.

Another way BASIC may be able to specify a double-precision variable is by using a type declaration symbol. Some versions use the letter D; others use the pound sign (#).

EXAMPLE:

```
10   A# = 11.41596283746
20   F# = 2.345345345345D-5
```

● **Loops:** It is often necessary to write a program in which the same portions are performed not just once but a number of times. Where a given action is done a multitude of times, a programming device named the LOOP is used in order to write a simplified program using as few statement lines as possible.

To demonstrate the simplicity and shortness of the loop technique, two sample program will be given. Both will solve the same problem, but the latter will use the loop technique.

Let's assume we need a table of the first 100 numbers plus their natural logs. Without a loop technique the program would be written as follows:

```
10     PRINT 1, LOG(1)
20     PRINT 2, LOG(2)
30     PRINT 3, LOG(3)
40     ..........
       ..........
       ..........
970    PRINT 97, LOG(97)
980    PRINT 98, LOG(98)
990    PRINT 99, LOG(99)
1000   PRINT 100, LOG(100)
1010   END
```

The above program would require 101 lines of code. Yet using the loop technique only five lines are required.

```
10     LET J = 1
20     PRINT J, LOG(J)
```

```
30    LET J = J + 1
40    IF J < = 100 THEN 20
50    END
```

By using the FOR-TO statement, we can further cut down the number of lines for four.

```
10    FOR J = 1 TO 100
20    PRINT J, LOG(J)
30    NEXT J
40    END
```

We can also have loops within loops. See *Nested Loops.*

● **Machine Language:** Machine language is the actual list of instructions that the computer understands. All computer languages, including BASIC, are translated into the machine language of the computer being used by its compiler, or interpreter.

A program written on one computer will therefore run on another computer (assuming we are using the same language, such as BASIC, LISP, or some other high-level language), but the languages themselves will only run on the same type of computer. There are so many versions of BASIC, for example, because each and every different computer requires that the language be written in its own machine codes.

● **MARGIN:** The MARGIN statement consists of the keyword MARGIN followed by a variable or a number. This statement controls or changes the maximum line length produced by output statements to "N" characters. When "N" is reached, an automatic carriage return/line feed is generated. That is, except for the difference in line length, the output operation remains the same.

EXAMPLE:

```
10    MARGIN N
20    MARGIN K−J
30    MARGIN 72
```

● **MAT CON:** The MAT CON is used to assign a value of one to each element of a given matrix.

EXAMPLE:

10   MAT J = CON

(where J is a matrix previously dimensioned).

Example of the MAT CON statement:

$$J = \begin{bmatrix} 1 & 1 & 1 \\ 1 & 1 & 1 \end{bmatrix}$$

If your BASIC doesn't contain the MAT CON statement, the following routine is an example of a MAT CON program written in BASIC. We will assume a 2-×-3 matrix as in the example. If the matrix you wish to set to all ones is of another size, the DIM statement, the loop sizes, and the variables will need to be changed to accommodate the different size.

EXAMPLE:

10   DIM J(2,3)
20   FOR I = 1 TO 2
30   FOR K = 1 TO 3
40   J(I,K) = 1
50   NEXT K
60 NEXT I

If your version of BASIC begins its arrays with a zero subscript (most do), some room in memory can be saved by letting the first loop run from 0 to 1, the second from 0 to 2, and the dimensions of the array can be set to 1,2 instead of 2,3. This small saving may not be worth it, however, because most people think of the upper left position of an array as 1,1 and not 0,0. You be the judge.

    ● **MAT IDN:** The MAT IDN statement assigns a value of zero to each element of a square matrix (Z-×-Z matrix) except those elements on the principal diagonal. The principal diagonal is the diagonal that runs from upper left to lower right, and a value of one will be assigned to each of its elements.

    A matrix that is assigned these values is known as an *identity matrix*.

EXAMPLE:

10   MAT J = IDN

(where J is a square matrix that has been previously dimensioned).

The identity matrix has an important characteristic: if a square matrix K is multiplied by the identity matrix J, then the product will be the square matrix K (K*J = J*K = K).

Example of an Identity Matrix:

$$J = \begin{bmatrix} 1 & 0 & 0 \\ 0 & 1 & 0 \\ 0 & 0 & 1 \end{bmatrix}$$

If your version of BASIC doesn't have the MAT IDN statement, a BASIC routine can be used to accomplish the same function. As in the MAT CON definition, the following routine does the MAT IDN function, this time for a 3- × -3 matrix similar to the other example:

EXAMPLE:
```
10   DIM J(3,3)
20   FOR I = 1 TO 3
30   FOR K = 1 TO 3
40   J(I,K) = 0
50   IF I = K THEN J(I,K) = 1
60   NEXT K
70   NEXT I
```

In this routine, all the elements are set to zero. Line 50 tests to see if the element is on the diagonal, and if so, that element is set equal to one.

For other size identity matrices, the DIM statement and the ranges of both loops must be changed to fit.

● **MAT INPUT (Matrix):** Some versions of BASIC allow the MAT INPUT statement to enter matrix elements as well as vector elements. With a matrix, however, the number of data elements to be entered must always be specified with the MAT INPUT statement.

● **MAT INPUT (Vector):** The MAT INPUT statement in BASIC is used to enter vector elements directly from an input terminal.

EXAMPLE:

10   MAT INPUT J

Most versions of BASIC only allow one vector to appear in a MAT INPUT statement.

When the MAT INPUT statement is executed by the computer a question mark (?) will appear at the start of a new line, indicating a request for data. Execution of the program will be suspended until the user types in the required vector elements, separated by commas. The first element entered will be assigned to $J(1)$, the second to $J(2)$, and so forth (assuming that J is the vector name). The zeroth element of the vector will be ignored.

After the user has finished entering the data, the user must depress the RETURN key, indicating to the computer to continue execution.

Any number of elements may be entered, provided that the number of data elements does not exceed the maximum number of vector elements, as specified by the DIM statement for that particular vector name.

This statement does not exist in many versions of BASIC. If needed, a routine may be written in BASIC to perform the same function, as follows:

EXAMPLE:

```
10   DIM J(ROWS,COLS)
20   FOR I = 1 TO ROWS
30   FOR K = 1 TO COLS
40   PRINT "VALUE FOR ROW";I;", COL";K
50   INPUT J(I,K)
60   NEXT K
70   NEXT I
```

If the number of data elements is too great for one line, subsequent lines may be used if each line to be extended ends in an ampersand (&). The ampersand must therefore appear after the last data element in each line except the last. A new question mark will be printed at the start of a new line if the ampersand was used to terminate the previous line.

EXAMPLE:

?1,4,−5,8,9,−23,4,18,28&
?8,7,−2,17,8,11,−10,19,30,47

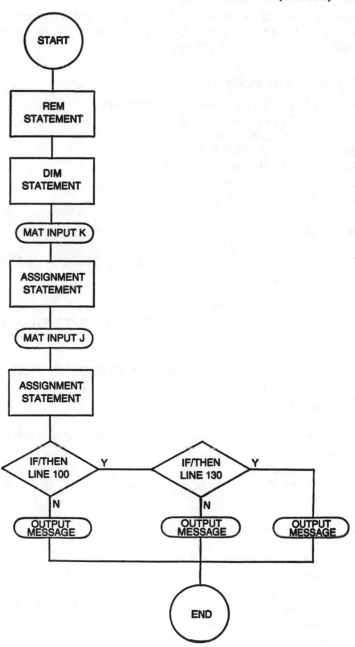

Flowchart for MAT INPUT statement.

If the vector was dimensioned for 50 elements and only 20 elements have been entered, the vector elements X(21) to X(50) will not be affected by the MAT INPUT statement.

PROGRAMMING EXAMPLE:

```
10    REM THIS PROGRAM DEMONSTRATES THE
20    REM MAT INPUT STATEMENT
30    DIM K(100),J(100)
40    PRINT "ENTER K VALUES"
50    MAT INPUT K
60    LET K1 = NUM
70    PRINT "ENTER J VALUES"
80    MAT INPUT J
90    LET J1 = NUM
100   IF K1 < > J1 THEN 130
110   PRINT "THE NUMBER OF J AND K ELEMENTS ARE
      THE SAME"
120   GOTO 170
130   IF K1 > J1 THEN 160
140   PRINT "THERE ARE MORE J ELEMENTS THAN K
      ELEMENTS"
150   GOTO 170
160   PRINT "THERE ARE MORE K ELEMENTS THAN J
      ELEMENTS"
170   END
```

● **MAT INV:** If we calculate the inverse of a square matrix, we generate a square matrix for which the product and its inverse are equal to the identity matrix.

Therefore, if J is the original matrix and K is its inverse, we have:

$$J*K = K*J = L$$

where L is the identity matrix.

A matrix must be square for its inverse to be defined, but it is not possible to calculate an inverse for all matrices that are square.

To calculate the inverse, if it exists, we use the MAT INV statement.

EXAMPLE:

```
10    MAT J = INV(K)
```

(where K is the original matrix and J is assigned the inverse of K. Both J and K must be previously dimensioned.)

● **MAT PRINT:** In BASIC the MAT PRINT statement is used to print the elements of a vector or a matrix.

EXAMPLE:
```
10   MAT PRINT J
20   MAT PRINT K
```

In the previous example, J and K may either be vectors or matrices. The elements of J for example will be printed in columnar form if J is a vector, and in table form if J is a matrix. As with the MAT READ statement, the zeroth elements will be ignored. When the MAT PRINT statement is operating on a matrix, each element of each row will be widely spaced, with a maximum of 5 elements per line. Therefore, in the cases of large matrices, several lines may be required for each row. A blank line will appear between successive rows.

The following rules always apply:

A) MATRICES
   1) Following a matrix name with a comma will have no effect on the spacing of the output.
   2) Following a matrix name with a semicolon will cause the elements of the rows of the matrix to be printed with a minimum of spacing between the elements. Successive rows will be separated by a blank line.
B) VECTORS
   1) If a vector name is followed by a comma, then the elements will be printed in row form rather than columnar form. Wide separation (maximum 5 elements per row) will be used.
   2) If a vector name is followed by a semicolon, then the elements of the vector will be printed in row form with minimum spacing between them.

Several vectors or matrices can appear in the same MAT PRINT statement if desired. Array names must be separated by commas or semicolons. The output will be determined by the type of punctuation following each array name.

The MAT PRINT statement can contain only matrix and vec-

tor names. Function references and formulas are not permitted.
The following are valid MAT PRINT statements:

```
10      MAT PRINT A
20      MAT PRINT A,
30      MAT PRINT A;
40      MAT PRINT A,B
50      MAT PRINT A;B
60      MAT PRINT A,B;
70      MAT PRINT A;B;
80      MAT PRINT A,B,K;J;
```

If your version of BASIC doesn't have the MAT PRINT statement, it can be simulated by the same technique as given under
the definition for MAT INPUT. A routine for printing a 3-×-3
matrix could be written:

EXAMPLE:

```
10   DIM J(3,3)
.
.
.
200  FOR I = 1 TO 3
210  FOR J = 1 TO 3
220  PRINT J(I,J)
230  NEXT J
240  NEXT I
```

The values for J are calculated and placed into the matrix
elsewhere in the program, before lines 200-240 are executed.

● **MAT READ:** In BASIC the MAT READ statement
is used to enter values for the elements of a vector or matrix. This
statement is used in conjuction with DATA statements.

EXAMPLE:

```
10    MAT READ K
```

(where K is a vector or matrix that has already been dimensioned).
When the computer executes a MAT READ statement, the set
of elements in the DATA statements are assigned to the elements

of the matrix, beginning with the subscript 1.

In versions of BASIC that permit a zero subscript, the elements, with subscript zero will be ignored. That is, the following elements will not be assigned values from a MAT READ statement: Y(0,0), Y(X,0), Y(0,X). Therefore, whenever you are using matrices in a version of BASIC that allows zero subscripts, never use zeros, because the first element in a vector or matrix is always 1, not 0.

A single MAT READ statement may contain more than one matrix or vector.

EXAMPLE:

10   MAT READ X, Y, Z

(where X, Y, Z are previously dimensioned.)

EXAMPLE:

10   DIM X(3,3)
.
.
.
200   FOR I = 1 TO 3
210   FOR J = 1 TO 3
220   READ X(I,J)
230   NEXT J
240   NEXT I

The example is for a 3-×-3 matrix. Lines 10, 200, and 210 must be changed for other size matrices; if a 5-×-5 matrix is to be read, each 3 in these lines must be changed to a 5.

● **MAT TRN:** In BASIC the MAT TRN statement causes the rows of columns of a given matrix to be interchanged or transposed.

EXAMPLE:

10   MAT(J) = TRN(K)

(where K is an M-×-N matrix and J is the generated N-×-M matrix. Both J and K must be previously dimensioned.)

The elements are related as follows:

$$J(I,L) = K(L,I)$$

and matrix J is termed the transpose of the Matrix K.

EXAMPLE:

$$If K = \begin{bmatrix} 1 & 8 & 10 \\ 4 & 7 & 3 \end{bmatrix}$$

then 10 MAT J = TRN(K) will generate

$$J = \begin{bmatrix} 1 & 4 \\ 8 & 7 \\ 10 & 3 \end{bmatrix}$$

As we can see the Nth row of K becomes the Nth column of J, and the Nth column of K becomes the Nth row of J.

To simulate this function in BASIC where it is needed but not available, try the following routine:

EXAMPLE:
```
 10   DIM K(2,3)
  .
  .
  .
200   FOR I = 1 TO 2
210   FOR L = 1 TO 3
220   J(L,I) = K(I,L)
230   NEXT L
240   NEXT I
```

In this example, it is assumed that the values of the elements of the matrix K have been stored or read in prior to the transpose operation. For matrices of other sizes, the counters for the loops and the DIM sizes will need changing (similar to the example at the end of the *MAT READ* definition).

● **Matrix Addition:** To carry out matrix addition, the MAT addition statement form is used.

EXAMPLE:

```
10    MAT K = J + L
```

The result of this MAT statement is that each element of K is assigned the sum of the corresponding elements of J and L. Thus K(1,3) = J(1,3) + L(1,3).

Note: The two matrices being added must have the same number of rows and columns.

If J and L are both 2-×-3 matrices, whose elements are

$$J = \begin{bmatrix} 1 & 3 & 5 \\ 2 & 4 & 6 \end{bmatrix} \quad L = \begin{bmatrix} 3 & 5 & 1 \\ 2 & 3 & 4 \end{bmatrix}$$

the MAT statement

10   MAT K = J + L

will cause K to be a 2-×-3 matrix whose elements are

$$K = \begin{bmatrix} 4 & 8 & 6 \\ 4 & 7 & 10 \end{bmatrix}$$

A matrix may be updated by the following procedure:

10 MAT K = K + J

but multiple sums are not permissible; that is,

10   MAT K = K + J + L

would not be allowed.

To add two 4-×-4 matrices when your BASIC does not have the built-in MAT functions, try this routine:

EXAMPLE

```
10    DIM J(4,4),L(4,4),K(4,4)
  .
  .
  .
200   FOR M = 1 TO 4
210   FOR N = 1 TO 4
220   K(M,N) = J(M,N) + L(M,N)
```

```
230   NEXT N
240   NEXT M
```

Here. the two 4-×-4 matrices J and L are added and their sum stored in the 4-×-4 matrix K. The values for the elements of J and L are assumed to have been previously assigned, as in MAT READ or the like. Matrices of other sizes can be added in the same way; be sure to change the DIM statement and the upper values for the loop variables.

● **Matrix Assignment:** To assign the matrix A to matrix B the MAT assignment statement is used.

EXAMPLE:
```
10    MAT J = K
20    MAT L = P
30    MAT H = G
```

In the case of MAT J = K, each element of K is assigned to the corresponding element of J.

Thus if K is the following 2-×-3 matrix

$$K = \begin{bmatrix} 1 & 5 & 8 \\ -4 & 6 & -9 \end{bmatrix}$$

the statement

```
10    MAT J = K
```

will cause J to be 2-×-3 matrix whose elements are

$$J = \begin{bmatrix} 1 & 5 & 8 \\ -4 & 6 & -9 \end{bmatrix}$$

To reference any element in J we use subscript variables. Thus the value 6 would have been referenced as J(2,2).

If not available in your BASIC, here is an example of a routine that will assign each element of matrix K to the corresponding matrix J.

EXAMPLE:

```
10   DIM K(2,3),J(2,3)
.
.
.
200  FOR I = 1 TO 2
210  FOR L = 1 TO 3
220  J(I,L) = K(I,L)
230  NEXT L
240  NEXT I
```

It is assumed that the values for the elements of K have been assigned prior to line 200. For matrices of other sizes, remember to alter the DIM and FOR-TO sizes accordingly.

● **Matrix Multiplication:** Two matrices may be multiplied if the number of columns in the first matrix is the same as the number of rows in the second matrix. The result of matrix multiplication is the generation of a matrix having the same number of rows as the first matrix and the same number of columns as the second matrix.

Therefore, if K is a 3-×-5 matrix and J is a 5-×-9 matrix, then the operation L = K*J will generate the L matrix having three rows and 9 columns.

Each element of L will be obtained as follows:

$$L(I,M) = K(I,1)*J(1,M) + K(I,2)*J(2,M) + K(I,3)*J(3,M)$$

Matrix multiplication is carried out in the following statement:

```
10     MAT L = K*J
```

Note: A matrix cannot be updated by means of the matrix multiplication statement.

In BASIC where the MAT statement isn't available, a routine for matrix multiplication can be written to simulate this function.

EXAMPLE:

```
10   DIM K(3,5),J(5,9),L(3,9)
.
.
.
```

```
200   FOR I = 1 TO 3
210   FOR M = 1 TO 9
220   L(I,M) = K(I,1)*J(I,M) + K(I,2)*J(2,M) + K(I,3)*J(3,M)
230   NEXT M
240   NEXT I
```

In this example, it is assumed that the values for the elements of the matrices K and J have already been assigned as outlined under the *MAT READ* and *MAT INPUT* statements, or by a similar method. Changes in the DIM and FOR-TO values are needed for different-sized matrices. Line 220 must be altered accordingly.

● **Matrix Subtraction:** The matrix subtraction statement and the matrix addition statement are very similar except for the sign of operation. Thus the matrix subtraction statement takes the form:

10   MAT K = J−L

Each element of K is assigned the difference of the corresponding values of J and L. Therefore:

K(1,3) = J(1,3) − L(1,3)

The two matrices must have the same number of rows and columns.

If J and L are both 2-×-3 matrices whose elements are:

$$J = \begin{bmatrix} 1 & 3 & 5 \\ 2 & 4 & 6 \end{bmatrix} \qquad L = \begin{bmatrix} 3 & 5 & 1 \\ 2 & 3 & 4 \end{bmatrix}$$

the MAT statement

10 MAT K = J− L

will cause K to be a 2-×-3 matrix whose elements are:

$$K = \begin{bmatrix} -2 & -2 & 4 \\ 0 & 1 & 2 \end{bmatrix}$$

A matrix may be updated as follows:

10   MAT K = K−J

This statement may be simulated, if not available in your BASIC, in the same way as given under *Matrix Addition.* Change the + sign in line 220 to a −.

● **MAT ZER:** In BASIC the MAT ZER statement is used to assign a value of zero to each element of a given matrix.

EXAMPLE:

10   MAT J = ZER

(where J is a matrix previously dimensioned.)

Example of the MAT ZER statement:

$$J = \begin{bmatrix} 0 & 0 & 0 \\ 0 & 0 & 0 \end{bmatrix}$$

This statement can be simulated in BASIC by using the routine given in the *MAT IDN* definition, omitting line 50.

● **MID$:** The library function MID$ occurs in two types: one with two arguments and the other with three arguments.

    A) Two argument MID$ returns characters from the string expression X$ starting at character position N.
    B) Three argument MID$ returns M characters from the string expression X$ starting at the Nth character.

EXAMPLES:

10   PRINT MID$(X$,N)
20   PRINT MID$(J$,4)
30   PRINT MID$(K$,N,M)
40   PRINT MID$(K$,11,4)

PROGRAMMING EXAMPLE:

10   REM THIS PROGRAM DEMONSTRATES
20   REM THE MID$ FUNCTION

```
30    INPUT J$
40    FOR N = 1 TO LEN(J$)
50    PRINT MID$(J$,N,1), MID$(J$,N,2)
60    NEXT N
70    END
```

RUN

```
?BASIC
B   BA
A   AS
S   SI
I   IC
C   C
```

END

Some versions of BASIC allow the use of the MID$ statement on the left side of the equal sign.

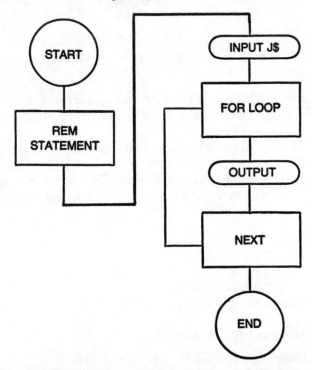

Flowchart for MID$ function.

EXAMPLE:

200 MID$ (X$,11,1) = "&"

When used this way, the eleventh character of the variable X$ is changed to the character "&". If allowed, it is another way to modify a string variable besides LEFT$, RIGHT$, and concatenation.

● **Mode:** In BASIC, mode may be thought of as a description of a switch. Changing the mode is comparable to rotating or toggling a switch to a different position. Each position changes the way a certain operation will be carried out. In the trig functions, mode refers to which format is being used: radians, grads, or degrees. The SET command is the controller of the "mode" switch. If we set radians, all trig functions following the SET command (SET RAD) will be in radians.

In some versions of BASIC, the mode may be thought of as the function the computer is performing at the moment. Four common modes are:

1. Immediate Mode: For typing in program lines or for executing an instruction immediately, such as PRINT 2 + 2. Note there is no line number; so the computer immediately responds with 4.
2. Execution Mode: The computer is executing instructions or a program.
3. Edit Mode: For changing the contents of a program line.
4. System Mode: For loading or executing machine-language programs.

● **Multiline Functions:** Many calculations cannot be carried out using a single statement, as when lengthy formulas or conditional branching operations are to be carried out. The multiline function format is ideally suited for calculations, complex or lengthy. Like a single-line function, a multiline function can have any number of dummy arguments but can return only one value.

The format is as follows: the first statement must be a DEF FN statement but, unlike a single-line function, the multiline function definition is not included in the DEF FN statement. The last statement must be the FNEND (function end) statement, and consists merely of the keyword FNEND.

Between the DEF FN and FNEND statements any number of

other statements may occur, but at least one must be an assignment statement (LET).

EXAMPLE:

```
10      DEF FNC(J,K,L)
20      ..........
30      ..........
40      LET FNC = (J*K*L)/J–K
50      FNEND
```

The grammatical rules are the same as those of the single line function:

1) A function definition can appear anywhere in a program.
2) A function is referenced by specifying its name, followed by a list of arguments enclosed in parentheses and separated by commas.
3) Control cannot be transferred between a statement within a function and a point external to the function.

The function reference may be nested, with the level of nesting depending on the version of BASIC being used.

EXAMPLE:

```
10      DEF FNZ(J,K)
20      LET FNZ = J
30      IF J < K THEN 50
40      LET FNZ = K
50      FNEND
60      ..........
70      ..........
80      ..........
90      PRINT FNZ(FNZ(A,B),FNZ(B,C))
```

VARIABLES other than those specified as arguments may appear in a multiline function, just as they may be found in a single-line function.

● **Multiple Branching:** In BASIC the ON-GOTO statement carries out the function of multiple branching. This statement includes a variable or a formula and a list of remote statements. Control is passed to the first remote statement if the variable or formula equates to 1, to the second if the variable or formula is equal to 2, and so forth.

EXAMPLE:

```
10    ON J GOTO 100, 350, 900, 45
20    ON K—J GOTO 46, 18, 28
30    ON B*A GOTO 1000, 1500, 3010
```

If the variable or formula has a value that is not integral, then the decimal portion will be truncated. **Note:** Many versions of BASIC allow the interchange of the keywords GOTO and THEN.

EXAMPLE:

```
10    ON J*K THEN 150, 200, 100, 260
```

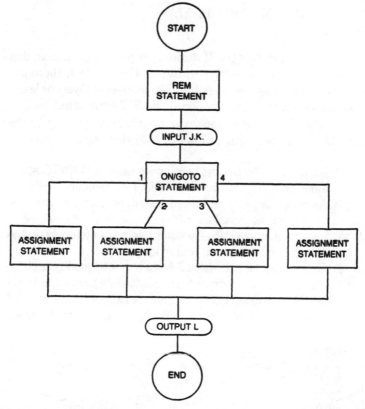

Flowchart for ON/GOTO statement.

PROGRAMMING EXAMPLE:

```
10     REM THIS PROGRAM DEMONSTRATES THE
20     REM ON-GOTO STATEMENT
30     PRINT "ENTER 1 FOR SQUARE ROOT, 2 FOR"
40     PRINT "LOG, 3 FOR SINE AND 4 FOR COSINE"
50     PRINT "ENTER ARGUMENT AFTER OPTION"
60     INPUT J,K
70     ON J GOTO 80, 100, 120, 140
80     LET L = SQR(K)
90     GOTO 150
100    LET L = LOG(K)
110    GOTO 150
120    LET L = SIN(K)
130    GOTO 150
140    LET L = COS(K)
150    PRINT
160    PRINT "SOLUTION IS ";L
170    END
```

● **Nested Loops:** If desired, loops may be nested; that is, one loop may be imbedded within another. In fact, there can be several layers or levels of nesting. The number of layers or levels of nesting depends on the version of BASIC being used.

When writing nested loops, the restrictions applying to the FOR-TO-NEXT loop apply, plus the following requirements:

1) Each nested loop must begin with its own FOR-TO statement and end with its own NEXT statement.
2) An outer loop and an inner (nested) loop cannot have the same running variable.
3) Loops cannot overlap. An inner loop must be totally nested or imbedded within an outer loop.
4) Control can be transferred from a nested loop to a statement in an outer loop or to a remote statement completely outside the nest. However control cannot be transferred from a remote statement outside the nest into the nest.

EXAMPLE:

```
10     FOR J = 1 TO K
20     ..........
30     ..........
40     FOR L = 1 TO M
```

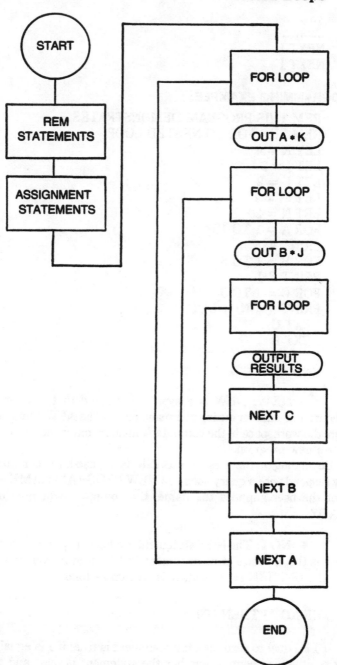

Flowchart for Nested Loop.

```
50    ..........
60    ..........
70    NEXT L
80    NEXT J
```

PROGRAMMING EXAMPLE:

```
10    REM THIS PROGRAM DEMONSTRATES
20    REM THE FOR TO NESTED LOOP
30    LET K = 4
40    LET J = 3
50    LET L = 2
60    LET M = 10
70    LET N = 20
80    FOR A = 1 TO 10
90    PRINT A*K
100   FOR B = 1 TO 5
110   PRINT B*J
120   FOR C = 1 TO 5
130   PRINT ((M*N) + L)/C
140   NEXT C
150   NEXT B
160   NEXT A
170   END
```

● **NEW:** NEW is a system command that is entered without a line number during command mode. The NEW command clears the workspace in the computer's main memory and prepares it for a new program.

Depending on the version of BASIC being used, the computer may respond with a query such as "NEW PROGRAM NAME—". After the user supplies the name, the computer will type out READY.

● **NOT:** The NOT statement is a logical operator whose result is the opposite of its argument. When used in conjunction with the IF-THEN statement, it is written as follows:

```
10    IF NOT J THEN 600
```

If J is equal to zero then the statement is true; if J is equal to any positive or negative number the statement is false and the branch to 600 will not occur.

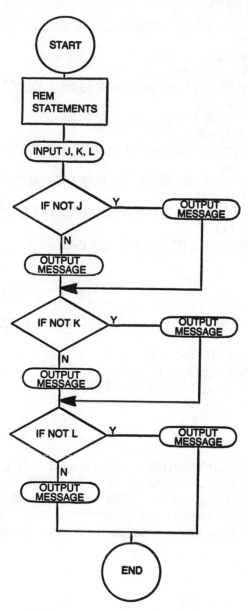

Flowchart for NOT function.

PROGRAMMING EXAMPLE:

```
10   REM THIS PROGRAM DEMONSTRATES
20   REM THE NOT FUNCTION
```

```
30    PRINT "ENTER 3 NUMBERS, 1 OF WHICH SHOULD BE
      ZERO"
40    INPUT J,K,L
50    IF NOT J THEN 80
60    PRINT "THE FIRST NUMBER IS NOT ZERO"
70    GOTO 90
80    PRINT "THE FIRST NUMBER IS ZERO"
90    IF NOT K THEN 120
100   PRINT "THE SECOND NUMBER IS NOT ZERO"
110   GOTO 130
120   PRINT "THE SECOND NUMBER IS ZERO"
130   IF NOT L THEN 160
140   PRINT "THE THIRD NUMBER IS NOT ZERO"
150   GOTO 170
160   PRINT "THE THIRD NUMBER IS ZERO"
170   END
```

RUN

```
ENTER 3 NUMBERS, 1 OF WHICH SHOULD BE ZERO
?11,0,−8
THE FIRST NUMBER IS NOT ZERO
THE SECOND NUMBER IS ZERO
THE THIRD NUMBER IS NOT ZERO
```

END

● **NUM:** The NUM function is used to determine how many values have been entered via a MAT INPUT statement. Whenever the library function NUM is referenced, it returns the number of data elements entered only by the most recent MAT INPUT statement. An argument for this function is not required.

EXAMPLE:

```
10    LET J(0) = NUM
20    PRINT J(0);"ELEMENTS"
```

As can be seen by this example, it is convenient to use the zero element of the vector in the assignment statement using the NUM function.

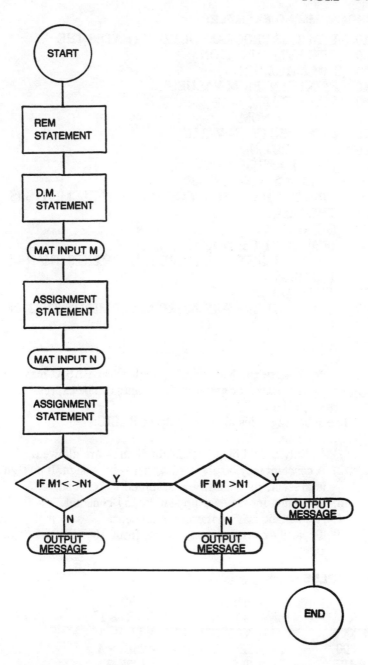

FLOWCHART for NUM function.

PROGRAMMING EXAMPLE:

```
10    REM THIS PROGRAM DEMONSTRATES THE
20    REM NUM FUNCTION
30    DIM M(100),N(100)
40    PRINT "ENTER M VALUES"
50    MAT INPUT M
60    LET M1 = NUM
70    PRINT "ENTER N VALUES"
80    MAT INPUT N
90    LET N1 = NUM
100   IF M1 < > N1 THEN 130
110   PRINT "THE NUMBER OF M AND N ELEMENTS IS
      THE SAME
120   GOTO 170
130   IF M1 > N1 THEN 160
140   PRINT "THERE ARE MORE N ELEMENTS THAN M
      ELEMENTS"
150   GOTO 170
160   PRINT "THERE ARE MORE M ELEMENTS THAN N
      ELEMENTS
170   END
```

● **Numbers:** Numerical quantities in BASIC may be referred to as *constants* or *numbers*. Constants can be expressed as integers or decimals.

The following rules always apply in BASIC:

1) Usually only 8 or 9 significant figures are allowed.
2) A constant may be prefixed with a − or + sign. If no sign is present, the quantity is assumed to be positive.
3) A comma must never appear in any constant.
4) A constant may contain an exponent.
5) Typically constants may range from 10^{-99} through 0 to 10^{99}.

EXAMPLES (each row is valid):

0	+0	-0
1	+1	0.1E + 1
+2000	2000	2.0E + 3
-2500	-2.5E + 3	-.25E + 4
+.125	1.25E-1	125E-3
100000	1E5	1E + 5

Most versions of BASIC have rules for deciding which kinds of numbers are being processed and stored. There are usually two kinds of numbers: real and decimal. In addition, there are alternate ways that these two kinds of numbers can be expressed: single precision, double precision, and scientific or exponential. See *Precision* and *Long*.

● **ON-GOSUB:** In BASIC, the ON-GOSUB statement carries out the function of multiple branching to subroutines. This statement includes a variable or a formula and a list of remote GOSUBs. The first subroutine is called if the variable or formula equals 1, the second if the variable or formula is equal to 2, and so forth.

EXAMPLE:
```
10    ON J GOSUB 100,350,900,45
20    ON K-J GOSUB 46,18,28
30    ON B*A GOSUB 1000,1500,3010
```

If the variable or formula has a value that is not integral, the decimal portion will be truncated.

PROGRAMMING EXAMPLE:
```
10    REM THIS PROGRAM DEMONSTRATES
20    REM THE ON-GOSUB STATEMENT
30    PRINT "ENTER A NUMBER FROM 1 TO 4"
40    INPUT J
50    IF J < 1 OR J > 4 THEN 170
60    ON J GOSUB 90,110,130,150
70    PRINT K
80    GOTO 30
90    K = J*10
100   RETURN
110   K = J/10
120   RETURN
130   K = EXP(J)
140   RETURN
150   K = LOG(J)
160   RETURN
170   END
RUN
```

```
ENTER A NUMBER FROM 1 TO 4
?1
10
ENTER A NUMBER FROM 1 TO 4
?2
0.20000
ENTER A NUMBER FROM 1 TO 4
?3
20.0855
ENTER A NUMBER FROM 1 TO 4
?4
1.38629
ENTER A NUMBER FROM 1 TO 4
?5
END
```

● **ON-GOTO:** See *Multiple Branching*.

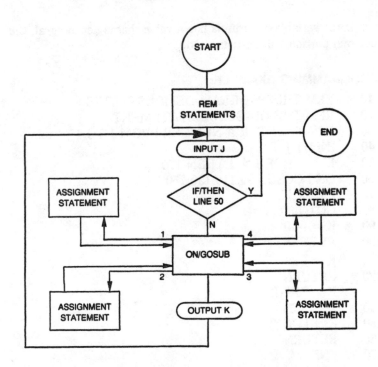

Flowchart for ON-GOSUB statement.

● **Operating Commands:** After initializing BASIC in whatever method is required for the computer system being used, BASIC will usually respond with some sort of prompting symbol. This prompting symbol or word indicates that the language is waiting for a command. The following are a list of typical operating (system) commands.

OLD: .... Loads a previously saved program. BASIC may request the name of the old program or file. This command is often called LOAD.

NEW: .... Allows the user to write a new program. BASIC may request a name for the program or file.

LIST: .... Prints the current program.

RUN: .... Executes the current program.

SAVE, RESAVE, or
REPLACE: .... Saves the current program.

UNSAVE, PURGE,
or SCRATCH: ..... Deletes the current program.

BYE, GOODBYE, or
SYSTEM: .... Exit from BASIC.

● **Operators:** Operators are special reserved symbols used by BASIC to indicate arithmetic operations.

These operators are:

Addition	$+$
Subtraction	$-$
Multiplication	$*$
Division	$/$
Exponentiation	$\uparrow$ or $\wedge$ (in some BASICS $**$)

Operators are used between numbers and numeric variables. Using operators in conjunction with numeric variables and numbers we can generate formulas.

EXAMPLES:

J + K
Q ↑ R*(Z −2)
X1-Z-B4
Z*(Z-1)/4
18-4

● **OR:** The OR statement is a logical operator, used to compare two operands. It may be used with either numerical or string variables or expressions.

If OR is used with numeric operands, the computer converts the operands to binary form and compares them bit by bit. For example, the operation 2 OR 4 yields 6, because in binary, 2 is 0010, 4 is 0100, and 6 is 0110.

OR is often used within IF-THEN statements, allowing the use of two or more qualifiers instead of only one. The IF-THEN is true if either or both of the qualifiers is true.

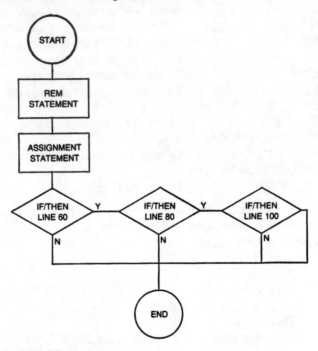

Flowchart for OR statement.

EXAMPLE:

10   IF X = 10 OR Y = 15 THEN 600

In this example, either the first qualifier (X = 10), or the second (Y = 15), or both must be true if the branch to 600 is to occur.

PROGRAMMING EXAMPLE:

10   REM THIS PROGRAM DEMONSTRATES THE

```
20      REM OR STATEMENT
30      LET K = 10
40      LET J = 20
50      LET L = 30
60      IF K = J/2 OR L = K + J THEN 80
70      STOP
80      IF J = L - K OR J = K*2 THEN 100
90      STOP
100     IF K = 10 OR J = 20 OR L = 30 THEN 120
110     STOP
120     END
```

● **Parentheses:** Parentheses are used to alter the normal hierarchy of operations in a formula. Since parentheses may be nested, they are evaluated from the innermost set outward. Inside each pair of parentheses, the normal hierarchical status is kept.

Note: Parentheses must always be used in pairs. Any imbalance between the number of left and right parentheses will cause an error condition.

For example, to evaluate the algebraic formula

$$[3.14(K + J)^5 + (19Y)^3] K/(J + 9)$$

it may be written in BASIC as

$$(3.14*(K + J) \uparrow 5 + (19*Y) \uparrow 3) * (K/(J + 9))$$

The introduction of extra parentheses in an equation will do no harm, but obviously the formula that uses the minimum number of parentheses is easier to read.

● **Password:** Some computer systems (usually large installations) require the user to enter a password to allow him access to the computer's facilities. The password may be numeric, a string, or a combination thereof. An illegal password will not allow the user to operate or use the computer.

EXAMPLE:
PASSWORD?
KEN
READY

94 Password

In this example, the password was accepted, but in the following the wrong password was used.

EXAMPLE:
PASSWORD?
PETER
ILLEGAL PASSWORD, TRY AGAIN
PASSWORD?

Generally the computer will allow the user three to four tries. After the fourth try, if the proper password has not been entered the connection to the terminal is turned off.

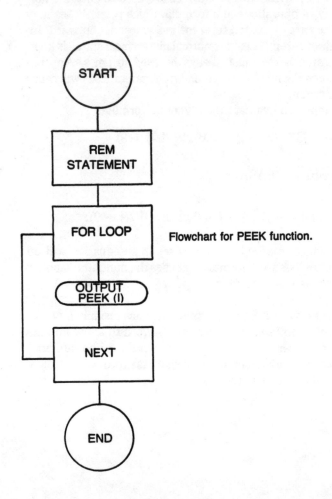

Flowchart for PEEK function.

● **PEEK:** The PEEK function in BASIC returns the contents of memory address (J). The value returned will be equal to or greater than 0 and less than or equal to 255. J must be in the range of 0 to 65535.

EXAMPLE:

```
10    PRINT PEEK(J)
20    PRINT PEEK(2819)
```

See *CALL*.

PROGRAMMING EXAMPLE:

```
10    REM THIS PROGRAM DEMONSTRATES
20    REM THE PEEK FUNCTION
30    FOR I = 300 TO 310
40    PRINT PEEK(I)
50    NEXT I
60    END
```

● **PI:** The library function PI returns the value of 3.1415926. It requires no argument.

EXAMPLE:

```
10    PRINT PI
20    PRINT PI*A
30    J = PI*K
```

● **POKE:** The POKE statement stores the byte specified by its second argument (J) into the location given by its argument (K). The byte to be stored must usually be equal to or greater than zero and less than or equal to 255. The location usually lies between zero and 65535. K and J must be separated by commas.

EXAMPLES:

```
10    POKE K,J
20    POKE 2560,130
30    POKE K, 250
```

Note: POKE stores directly into main memory. Care must be taken to see that important data is not overwritten by the POKE statement.

See *CALL*.

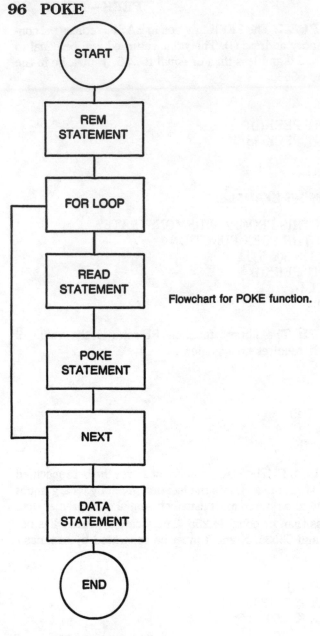

Flowchart for POKE function.

PROGRAMMING EXAMPLE:

```
10    REM THIS PROGRAM DEMONSTRATES THE
20    REM POKE FUNCTION
30    FOR I = 4001 TO 4010
```

```
40      READ N
50      POKE I,N
60      NEXT I
70      DATA 11,18,104,206,118,114,100,89,1,10
80      END
```

The numbers in the DATA statement are now stored, in order, in memory locations 4001 to 4010. Location 4001 contains the value 11; location 4002 contains the value 18, and so on.

A program of this type can be used to generate machine-language programs and subroutines. Obviously the data items in the DATA statements must correspond to the machine-language codes of the machine the BASIC program is running on.

● **Pointers and Counters:** A *pointer* is a number stored in a particular memory location. Its function is to store the location of an item of data; a certain record; the beginning, middle, or end of a list, and so on. The list could consist of individual numbers, personnel records, or even a machine-language program.

Some pointers are used to keep track of the status of a list, such as how many items have been read from a data list, or how many items are currently in a list. See *Random Data FilesPointer Control*.

A counter keeps track of how many times an operation has been carried out. The variable I in the following statement is a counter.

EXAMPLE:
FOR I - 1 TO 10

● **Precision:** Precision is the number of digits used in calculations in BASIC. Typically *single* precision offers 6 to 8 digits of accuracy in mathematical evaluations. *Double* precision offers twice as many digits, while *triple* precision offers three times as many numeric digits. Double or triple precision is used when greater than normal accuracy is required.

EXAMPLES:

Single precision:
345.786   (6 digits total)

Double precision:
6754998.75478   (12 digits total)

Triple precision:
345837658796546784   (18 digits total)

Most versions of BASIC allow the programmer to specify the precision of a particular number or numeric variable. If no precision is specified, the usual default is single precision.

Single precision may be specified most often by adding an exclamation point (!) to the end of the number. For example, 3.2!, 345.687!, and 0.003! are single-precision numbers.

To specify a number as double precision, there are at least three ways (your BASIC may have any or all):

1. Enter the number with more than the (default) number of digits. If your default single-precision number of digits is eight, then a number having more than eight digits may be treated by BASIC as a double-precision number.
2. Use a type declaration symbol. Many versions of BASIC use the pound sign (#), as a type declaration tag. If a number ends in this tag, such as 1234.123456789#, then BASIC is notified to store and process the number as double precision.
3. Some versions of BASIC also allow numbers expressed in scientific (exponential) notation to be labelled as double precision by placing the letter D in the proper position within the number. For example, 9.87612345D-5, 1.99999999999D + 3, and 1.00013456789D-12 are in double-precision scientific format.

Variables may also be specified as to type in similar ways. The most common variable typing conventions are:

1. Integer: Use the % sign. Examples: A%, R1%, INDEX%.
2. Single Precision: If no type specifier is used, the usual default type is single precision. If a type specifier is used, it is usually the ! symbol. Examples: A, R1, INDEX, A!, R1!, INDEX!.
3. Double Precision: Use the # sign. Examples: A#, R1#, INDEX#.

Some versions of BASIC permit mixed-type expressions, and other versions do not. If permitted, an expression like

$$A = B\#/C$$

will be processed. If not permitted, an error message may or may not occur.

● **PRINT:** The PRINT statement is used to transmit data (numeric or string) to the output device. This statement consists of the keyword PRINT and a list of the output data. The output data may be formulas, strings, or variables. Successive items must be separated by either commas or semicolons. Strings must be enclosed in quotation marks.

EXAMPLE:

```
10    PRINT "JANE", "KEN"
20    PRINT X; Y; Z
30    PRINT "HELLO"; A$
40    PRINT 9*X-4
```

The following rules always apply:

1) Each PRINT statement generates only one new line unless the list presented by the PRINT statement requires more than one line.
2) A PRINT statement containing no data items will produce a blank line.
3) In most versions of BASIC, an integer quantity that contains eight or less digits will be printed as an integer number. If an integer quantity exceeds eight digits, it will be rounded to six significant figures and printed as a decimal number with an exponent. A decimal quantity is printed as a decimal number. If the quantity contains more than six digits, it will be rounded to six digits. An exponent will be shown if the magnitude of the number exceeds 999999 or is less than 0.1 and contains more than six significant figures.
4) Strings must always be enclosed in quotation marks.
5) If the data items in a PRINT statement are separated by commas, each line of output will be divided into 5 zones of equal length. One output value will be printed per zone.
6) If a comma follows the last item in a PRINT statement, the first output from a subsequent PRINT statement will be printed on the same line if sufficient space permits.
7) Up to four commas may be placed in a PRINT statement consecutively. The effect of each comma is to space over one zone. With this method widely-spaced data may be achieved.

100 PRINT

8) If semicolons are used instead of commas to separate data items, no spaces will be left between items.
9) Placing a semicolon after the last data item in a PRINT statement causes the output of the next PRINT statement to occur on the same line without any spaces.

Variations are widespread among versions of BASIC in the use of these rules for PRINT statements. The number and effect of commas and the required or optional use of semicolons are things to watch for. Study your BASIC reference guide to compare these rules.

An often-used abbreviation for the keyword PRINT is the question mark. Instead of typing PRINT A, this shorthand form allows you to type ? A. The result is the same—the value of the variable A is printed on the output device.

Many versions of BASIC will convert the listing of the question mark into the keyword PRINT. If you type 10 ? A into the computer, and then list it, the listing will probably read: 10 PRINT A. The computer has recognized the abbreviation and displays the actual keyword.

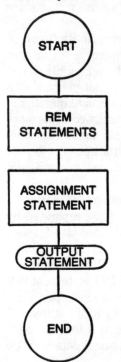

Flowchart for PRINT statement.

PROGRAMMING EXAMPLE:

```
10    REM THIS PROGRAM DEMONSTRATES THE PRINT
20    REM STATEMENT
30    LET K = 15
40    LET J = 10
50    PRINT
60    PRINT 1, 2, 3, 4, 5
70    PRINT
80    PRINT J, J*2, J*3, J*4, J*5
90    PRINT K, K*2, K*3, K*4, K*5
100   PRINT
110   PRINT "K TIMES J EQUALS"; K*J
120   PRINT "K LESS J EQUALS"; K-J
130   END
```

RUN

1	2	3	4	5
10	20	30	40	50
15	30	45	60	75

K TIMES J EQUALS 150
K LESS J EQUALS 5

END

● **PRINT USING:** The PRINT USING statement allows the user to output multiple fields of both strings and numerics, where the strings are enclosed in quotation marks. The usage can be readily understood by carefully reading the examples.

EXAMPLE:

```
10    LET A = 10.34
20    LET B = 5.06
30    LET C = 9.18
40    A$ = " $$###.## $$###.## $$###.##"
50    PRINT USING A$;A;B;C
```

This example produces the following output:

$10.34 $5.06 $9.18

Of course strings may be added to the PRINT USING statement. If we replace line 40 with:

40 A\$ = "THE AMOUNTS ARE: (A)##.##, (B)##.##,
         AND (C)##.##"

we obtain for an output the following:

THE AMOUNTS ARE: (A)10.34,(B)5.06;AND (C)9.18

Note: The commas, parentheses, numerics (if any), and strings will be reproduced in the output.

Thus we can see that the PRINT USING statement allows formatting of the output. It allows control over justification and spacing of the output.

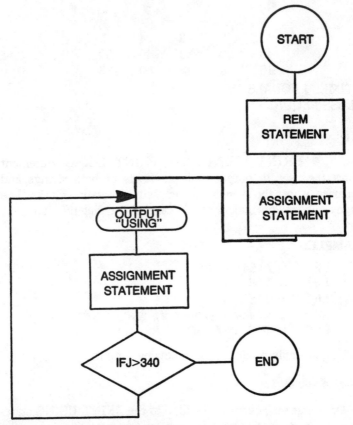

Flowchart for PRINT USING statement.

PROGRAMMING EXAMPLE:

```
10    REM THIS PROGRAM DEMONSTRATES
20    REM THE PRINT USING FUNCTION
30    LET J = 4.15
40    PRINT USING "####.##",J,"BACTERIA"
50    LET J = J*3
60    IF J > 340 THEN 80
70    GOTO 40
80    END
```

RUN

```
  4.15 BACTERIA
 12.45 BACTERIA
 37.35 BACTERIA
112.05 BACTERIA
336.15 BACTERIA
```

END

● **Program:** A program may be defined as a set of directions or instructions that tell a computer how to solve a problem. Any program (written in BASIC or any other computer language) must fulfill certain requirements.

1) It must be written in a language that is understood by the computer.
2) It must be written completely and precisely. A computer has no way to interpret what you "really" mean; it can only do what you tell it to do.

Regardless of the language being used, or the type of computer system being run on, each and every program consists of three basic sections:

1) The necessary information (the input data)
2) Processing of the input data
3) Output of the results obtained from the processing.

As with any formalized procedure, if mistakes occur in the program, you will undoubtedly end up with something other than desired for the output.

● ?(Question Mark): See *PRINT*.

● QUOTE: The QUOTE Statement is used to indicate to the BASIC program that the information being stored in a file is to be enclosed in quotation marks and will be red back at some time in the future by a BASIC program.

EXAMPLE:

```
10    QUOTE
20    QUOTE #2
```

In line 20 of this example, the #2 signifies that there is more than one set of information and that the quote refers to the second set only.

QUOTE: See *Sequential Data Files Writing*.

● **Random Data File:** A random data file contains individual data items that are not arranged in any particular order. With a random data file, each data item can be read directly from, or written directly onto, without proceeding sequentially along the data file from the beginning. Thus random is faster.

Note: In some versions of BASIC data files may consist of either string or numeric data but not both. The type of random file is specified with either a percent sign (%) for numeric files or a dollar sign ($) for string files. Usually a positive integer quantity (generally ranging from one to 132) must follow the $ sign. The positive integer quantity specifies the maximum number of characters that may appear in each string.

Random data files, unlike sequential data files, cannot be listed directly on a terminal device. The BASIC system commands cannot edit a random data file, but of course we can easily write a program which will handle these two problems.

● **Random Data File Creation:** Typical sequences of statements for random file creation follow the pattern of this routine:

EXAMPLE:

```
100   OPEN "FILENAME", 1
110   PRINT #1, A,B,C
120   CLOSE
```

There are almost as many variations of the random file creation process as there are computers, but the idea is much the same: open the file, write to it, close the file. The processes of opening and closing are used to tell BASIC which file you mean so your data doesn't end up in the wrong file.

Once the random file is created, the keywords PUT and GET are often used to store and retrieve data items.

● **Random Data File Pointer Control:** The data items in a random data file are not arranged in any special order, but the locations of the data items are numbered sequentially from the start of the file (beginning with number one) and are incremented by one for each consecutive data item. The concept of a pointer is used to indicate the location of any particular data file. The pointer must always be properly positioned before a data item can be transferred to or from (written to or read from) the data file.

EXAMPLE:

LOCATION	DATA ITEM
1	301049
2	21659
3	28
4	10
5	18
6	13718
7	8046
8	2091
9	18461
10	22964

The pointer is automatically advanced one location every time a data item is transferred to or from the data file. Therefore it is also possible to read or write data sequentially from a random data file. By using the SET statement (RESET in some versions of BASIC), we can reposition the pointer at any time.

Two library functions are closely related to the SET statement. They are the LOC and LOF functions. The LOF function indicates the last storage location in the file, while LOC allows us to determine the position of the pointer.

When using the SET statement we must also indicate which data channel is being used.

The format is to have the keyword SET followed by a colon

(as opposed to % in sequential files), followed by the channel number, then the location. The location may be specified by a formula, a variable, or a numeric constant, and must be separated by a comma from the channel number.

EXAMPLE:

```
10   SET:1,J
20   SET:3,4
```

Carefully study your BASIC reference manual for your particular computer. The keyword RESET is sometimes used for another function, or not used.

The keyword SET is not often used. Instead, a form of the GET statement performs the SET function of specifying the data channel, or *buffer number*.

● **Random Data File Reading:** In BASIC a random data file can be read either sequentially or randomly. The pointer position need not be considered if the data is to be read sequentially because the FILES statement places the pointer at the first location in the file and automatically advances one location each time a new data item is read.

If the items in a data file are to be read randomly, we must position the pointer to the proper location with the SET statement before attempting to read a particular data item.

EXAMPLES:
Sequential

```
10    FILES COUNTRIES$20
20    FOR M = 1 TO Z
30    READ:1,J$
40    PRINT J$
50    NEXT M
60    END
```

Random

```
10    FILES COUNTRIES$20
20    PRINT "LOCATION IN FILE"
30    INPUT K
40    SET:1,K
```

```
50    READ:1,J$
60    PRINT J$
70    GOTO 20
80    END
```

Variations of these statements are often found. They include:

Use of OPEN instead of FILES.
Use of INPUT# instead of READ.
Use of GET instead of SET and READ.

    ● **Random Data Files Reset Command:** See *Random Data Files Pointer Control.*

    ● **Random Data Files Set Command:** See *Random Data Files Pointer Control.*

    ● **Random Data File Writing:** In the same manner that a data item is read, a data item can be written onto a random file. Whereas with reading we use the READ statement, with writing we use the WRITE statement. The pointer must be positioned to the proper location before an entry can be written; also the new data item will replace the old data item previously stored in that location.

Variations will be encountered when programming to write to a random file. Some versions of BASIC use OPEN instead of FILES, GET instead of INPUT, and rely on the GET statement to eliminate the SET statement.

EXAMPLE:

```
10    FILES COUNTRIES$20
20    PRINT "WHICH LOCATION"
30    INPUT K
40    PRINT "DATA IS"
50    INPUT J$
60    SET:1,K
70    WRITE:1,J$
80    GOTO 20
90    END
```

    ● **RANDOMIZE:** The numbers generated by the RND library function are not truly random, as they are produced by a fixed computational procedure. They do, however, have the same statistical properties as do numbers which are truly random in nature. Numbers produced by random number generators are usually called pseudo-random numbers.

Every time a program which uses the RND function is run the same sequence of random numbers will be generated. For purposes of debugging, this reproducibility feature is very helpful, but most users would usually want different numbers each time the program is run.

The RANDOMIZE statement is used to ensure that a different sequence will be generated each time the program is run. The RANDOMIZE statement consists simply of the keyword RANDOMIZE. This function operates by providing a different starting point for the random number generator. Thus the RANDOMIZE statement must precede the first reference to the RND library function.

In other versions of BASIC, the keyword is RANDOM, RND(– TI), or RANDOMIZE TIMER. These keywords all have the same intent: to "reseed" the random number generator to provide a different sequence of random numbers.

EXAMPLE:

```
10    DIM K(50)
20    RANDOMIZE
30    ..........
40    FOR I = 1 TO 50
50    LET K(I) = RND
60    NEXT I
```

PROGRAMMING EXAMPLE:

```
10    REM THIS PROGRAM DEMONSTRATES
20    REM THE RANDOMIZE FUNCTION
30    RANDOMIZE
40    DIM J(100)
50    FOR I = 1 TO 100
60    J(I) = RND
70    NEXT I
80    FOR I = 1 TO 100
90    PRINT J(I)
100   NEXT I
110   END
```

● **READ-DATA:** When large numbers of data items are to be entered into the computer, the standard INPUT statement may be used, but this process can become time-consuming and tends to introduce errors. In such a case, the READ-DATA statement would be preferable. The READ-DATA statement is also the only way to introduce data in timesharing and single-user modes.

The READ statement specifies the variables whose values are to be entered into the computer via the program. This statement consists of the keyword READ followed by a list of input variables separated by commas. The list can contain ordinary numeric and/or string variables, or subscripted variables representing numeric and/or string variables.

The purpose of the DATA statement is to assign the appropriate values to the variables listed in the READ statement. The DATA statement consists of the keyword DATA followed by the list of numbers and/or strings, separated by commas. Of course each data entry in the DATA statement must correspond to a variable in the READ statement.

EXAMPLE:

```
10    READ L, K$, J$, X
20    DATA 100, KEN, JAYN, 150
```

All DATA statements, regardless of their position in the program, form a single DATA block. Each item in the DATA block maps (or corresponds) on a one-to-one basis to an appropriate variable in the READ statements. Actually this is not a true one-to-one correspondence as you may have more variables on one line of a READ statement than on one line of a DATA statement.

It should also be pointed out that in the following examples line 10 and line 20 are identical to line 30.

EXAMPLE:

```
10    DATA 5, HELLO, 36, 84
20    DATA FOX, HUNT, 82
30    DATA 5, HELLO, 36, 84, FOX, HUNT, 82
```

It is also to be remembered that the DATA specified by the READ-DATA statement are an integral part of the program as opposed to the INPUT statement.

Thus no matter how often the same program is run, the same data remains.

The following rules must be observed with a DATA block:

110   READY-DATA—Relational Operators

1) The DATA items must correspond in order (mapping) and in type to the variables specified by the READ statement.
2) There must be at least as many data elements in the DATA block as there are variables in the READ statements. Extra data will be ignored.
3) The elements in a DATA statement must be separated by commas. The last item in the DATA statement is *not* followed by a comma.
4) Elements of a DATA statement must be numeric or string in nature, not variables or formulas.
5) Strings containing commas or beginning or ending with blank spaces must be enclosed in quotation marks.
6) DATA statements should (but do not have to) be placed consecutively near the end of the program.

PROGRAMMING EXAMPLE:

```
5     REM DEMONSTRATES READ/DATA STATEMENTS
10    READ K,J,L,M
15    LET H = K*M-J*L
20    IF H = 0 THEN 65
30    READ P,Q
40    LET X = (P*M-J*Q)/H
45    LET Y = (K*Q-P*L)/H
50    PRINT X,Y
60    GOTO 30
65    PRINT "NO UNIQUE SOLUTION"
70    DATA 1,2,4
80    DATA 2,-7,5
90    DATA 1,3,4,-7
100   END
```

● **READY:** A BASIC-generated message indicating that the computer is waiting for a user command.

Alternate BASIC prompts include OK and no message at all except for a blinking dot or block.

● **Relational Operators:** Relational operators are used to form expressions or to compare two expressions.

The operator used to form an expression is the equal sign (=). The result of the use of this sign to form an expression is a change in the value of a variable or an assignment. The assignment statement is of the form LET A = 5, or LET F\$ = "NAME".

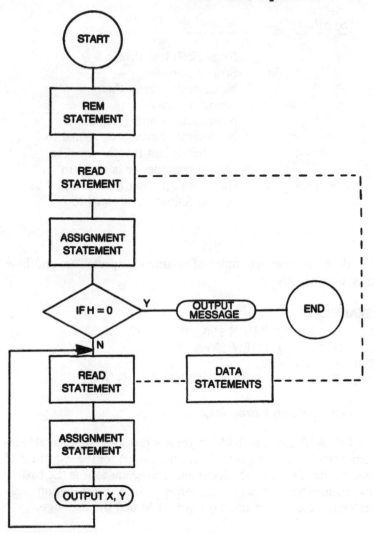

Flowcart for READ-DATA statement.

Examples of the change in the value of a variable are the line LET A = A + 15, the line F\$ = G\$ + V\$, or the line J\$ = H\$ + "COMPANY".

All the relational operators may be used to compare quantities, either strings or numerical quantities. They may be used in the FOR-NEXT and IF-THEN statements, and others.

Here is the list of relational operators:

Symbol	Meaning
<	Numerical: less than
	String: precedes
>	Numerical: greater than
	String: follows
=	Numerical or string: equal to
< > or ><	Numerical or string: not equal to
<= or =<	Numerical: less than or equal to
	String: precedes or is equal to
> = or =>	Numerical: greater than or equal to
	String: follows or is equal to

Here are some examples of relational expressions, and how they may be used:

EXAMPLE:

```
10    IF C$ > N$ THEN 100
10    IF A< = 1 THEN 100
230   FOR I = 1 TO 60
320   IF (A – 7)/2 < = X + 1 THEN G = G + 2
```

See *Conditional Branching*.

● **REM:** The REM statement provides no executable instructions for the computer. The chief reason for the use of REM statements is to properly document a program as it is the easiest way to introduce remarks (comments) into a BASIC program. This statement consists of the keyword REM and the message.

EXAMPLE:

10   REM THIS IS A PROGRAM

REM statements can be placed anywhere in a BASIC program. In some versions of BASIC it is also possible to include a remark on the same line as an ASSIGNMENT statement. To separate the remark from the rest of the statement an apostrophe must precede the remark.

The use of remarks (or comments) is important to programming in two ways. First, later updates and changes are much easier if the original program is well commented. Second, in the version of a program which is used often, comments will usually slow the

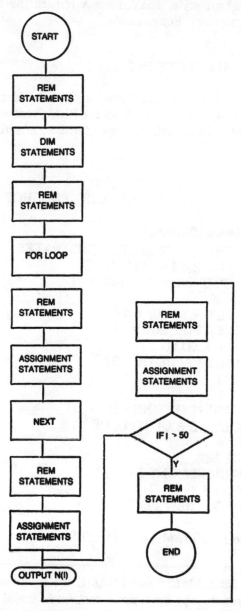

Flowchart for REM statement.

execution. The best compromise is to keep a well-remarked copy of the program in storage and to delete the comments from the version used daily.

A note about style: don't make a remark the target of a branching statement. For example:

```
10    GOTO 200
200   REM CALCULATE INTEREST
```

This method is bad form. Make line 200 the first line of the program section, and use line 199 for the REM. That way, line 199 can later be deleted for improved speed without affecting the flow of the program.

EXAMPLE:
```
10    LET K = J*A 'CALCULATE 1ST PRODUCT
```

PROGRAMMING EXAMPLE:
```
10    REM THIS PROGRAM DEMONSTRATES
20    REM THE REM STATEMENT
30    REM DIMENSION VARIABLE N
40    DIM N(50)
50    REM SET N(1 −50) = 1-50
60    REM IN A FOR LOOP
70    FOR I = 1 TO 50
80    REM SET VALUE OF N(I)
90    LET N(I) = I
100   NEXT I
110   REM PRINT OUT N(1-50)
120   REM USING A GOTO LOOP
130   LET I = 1
140   PRINT N(I)
150   REM INCREMENT I
160   LET I = I + 1
170   IF I > 50 THEN 200
180   GOTO 140
190   REM PROGRAM TERMINATES
200   END
```

● **RENAME:** The RENAME or REN command allows the user to rename a program that is contained currently in the computer's main memory work space.

The computer will generally respond to "RENAME" with "NEW PROGRAM NAME—", and the user then supplies the new name.

The command RENAME or NAME is used by some versions of BASIC to change the name of a disk file, instead of one in memory.

● **RESET:** In some versions of BASIC, RESET may be used as a command to close files and clear the buffer.

See *Random Data Files Pointer Control.*

● **RESTORE:** The correspondence between variables in the READ statement and the elements in the DATA statement is maintained by an internal pointer. The internal pointer indicates the next data element in the list to be read. In the case of strings and numerics, there are two pointers, one for each. Every time a data element is read the pointer is incremented.

If some or all of the data must be read again, the RESTORE statement is used. The RESTORE statement consists of the keyword RESTORE only. The use of this statement is to restore the pointer or pointers to the first data element or elements.

EXAMPLE:

```
10    READ J,K,L
20    ..........
30    ..........
40    RESTORE
50    READ M,N,P,Q
60    ..........
70    ..........
80    RESTORE
90    READ R,S
100   ..........
110   DATA 2,4,6,8,10,12,14
```

In the example given, J, K, and L are assigned the values of the first three elements. Using the RESTORE statement we can assign to M, N, P, and Q the first four values. If the RESTORE statement in line 80 was not present, M, N, P, and Q would have been assigned the "next" four values.

In most versions of BASIC using the RESTORE statement, an asterisk (*) or dollar sign ($) may be placed directly after the RESTORE keyword.

Other versions of BASIC may allow the use of a line number after the RESTORE keyword. In those cases, the data in that line, and the following lines may be READ again.

The asterisk indicates to the computer to restore only the numeric pointer, while the dollar sign indicates to restore only the string pointer.

EXAMPLE:

```
10    READ X,Y,Z,J$,K$
20    ..........
30    ..........
40    RESTORE*
50    READ H,I
60    ..........
70    ..........
80    READ L$
90    ..........
100   RESTORE $
110   READ A$,B$
120   ..........
130   DATA 10,20,30,MOUSE,RACCOON, SQUIRREL
```

In this example X, Y, and Z are assigned 10, 20, 30. H and I are assigned 10, 20 because of the RESTORE* in line 40. J$ and K$ are assigned MOUSE and RACCOON; then in line 80 L$ is assigned SQUIRREL. Since the RESTORE$ was not encountered until line 100, L$ was assigned the next string value. In line 110, A$ and B$ are assigned MOUSE and RACCOON, because this READ statement follows the RESTORE$ statement.

● **RESUME:** The RESUME statement is used in those versions of BASIC having error trapping and recovery capability. It is used to continue the execution of a program after an error has been trapped and handled. See *CONTINUE.*

● **RETURN:** The RETURN statement closes the subroutine procedure. When the computer encounters the keyword RETURN, control is transferred back to the statement following the point of reference. The RETURN statement consists of only the keyword RETURN.

Note: Control cannot be returned to the point of calling by other types of branching statements.

EXAMPLE:

```
10    LET K = 10
20    LET J = 20
30    GOSUB 80
40    ..........
50    PRINT Z
60    ..........
70    ..........
80    LET Z = J-K
90    RETURN
```

● **RIGHT$:** The library function RIGHT$ returns the rightmost N characters of the string expression X$.

EXAMPLES:

```
10    PRINT RIGHT$(X$,N)
20    PRINT RIGHT$(K$,6)
```

● **RND:** In BASIC, the RND library function is used to generate a random number. The function will return a different random number, with a value between zero and one, each time the function is referenced. Generally an argument is not required, but in some versions of BASIC, typically the integer-only versions, an argument is required. The RND function will then generate integer random numbers from 0 to the value of the argument.

EXAMPLE:

```
10    DIM K(50)
20    ..........
30    ..........
40    FOR I = 1 TO 50
50    LET K(I) = RND
60    NEXT I
```

This example will generate 50 random numbers. It should be remembered that the random function never generates a one, but a value very close to one.

To generate a random number between X and Y, the following formula may be used:

$$LET\ Z = X + (Y - X)*RND$$

EXAMPLE:

```
10     LET K = RND(J)
20     LET H = RND(10)
30     LET J = RND(28)
```

PROGRAMMING EXAMPLE:

```
10     REM THIS PROGRAM DEMONSTRATES
20     REM THE RND FUNCTION
30     PRINT "THIS PROGRAM ROLLS DICE"
40     LET J = INT(6*RND) + 1
50     LET K = INT(6*RND) + 1
60     PRINT "THE DICE ARE ";J;" AND ";K
70     END
```

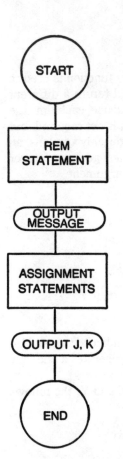

Flowchart for RND function.

● **RUN:** In most versions of BASIC, RUN can be used in either the command mode or inside the program as a statement. After loading a program in the command mode, the user types RUN and presses the Return or Enter key.

In either the command mode or as a program statement, the keyword RUN may have a line number as an argument. If specified, the program execution will begin with that line number.

The usual effect of a RUN command or statement is to clear all values of variables, and possibly CLOSE any files and reset some memory pointers. If you want to avoid the clearing, use GOTO line in the command mode, where *line* is the line number that you wish execution to begin. If you want the program to begin execution with line 320, use:

GOTO 320

Press Return or Enter, and execution will start. Be prepared for some error messages when doing this, though. If the computer encounters a DIM statement that has already been executed before the GOTO was issued, you'll get an error message. There is also the possibility of an error message if the values of variables are not correct for the starting line number, or if they are zero and should be nonzero.

● **SAVE:** After writing a program in BASIC the user can keep the program either on tape or on disc by using the SAVE command. The SAVE command usually requires the name of the program as an argument. Depending on the version of BASIC being used the user may be limited to the number of letters used in the name.

EXAMPLE:

SAVE,HEATLOSS
SAVE,INSULATION-FACTOR

After saving the program by name, the user can request the already written program by using the LOAD command.

● **Scalar Multiplication:** If all the elements of a given matrix are multiplied by a given constant, the operation of scalar multiplication is being carried out.

EXAMPLE:

10   MAT K = (J)*L

120 Scalar Multiplication

K and L are matrices, and J is an ordinary variable. Each element of K will be defined as K(I,J) = (J)*L(I,J).

If L is the following 2-×-3 matrix:

$$L = \begin{bmatrix} 1 & 3 & 5 \\ 2 & 4 & 6 \end{bmatrix}$$

and J = 2, then 10 MAT K = (2)*L where the elements of K are:

$$K = \begin{bmatrix} 2 & 6 & 10 \\ 4 & 8 & 12 \end{bmatrix}$$

The term within the parentheses need not be a single variable. Subscripted variables, constants, formulas, and function references may all be used, as long as the term represents a single numerical quantity. The scalar term must always be enclosed in parentheses.

The following are all valid scalar multiplication statements:

```
10   MAT K = (25)*L
20   MAT J = (Z*Y)*H
30   MAT L = (SQR(H-P))*B
```

Updating with scalar multiplication is as follows:

```
10   MAT K = (J)*K
```

If your version of BASIC doesn't have the Scalar Multiplication procedure, here's a simulation of the function.

EXAMPLE:
```
10   DIM L(2,3)
 .
 .
 .
100  FOR I = 1 TO 2
110  FOR J = 1 TO 3
120  K(I,J) = 2*L(I,J)
130  NEXT J
140  NEXT I
```

The values for the matrix L are assumed to have been put in

between lines 10 and 100 by the techniques given under MAT IN-PUT, MAT READ, or the equivalent thereof. The result of the routine is the matrix K whose elements are each twice that of the same-sized matrix L.

If a different-sized matrix is used, the DIM and FOR statements must be adjusted to suit.

● **SCRATCH:** The SCRATCH (SCR) command clears or erases the current contents of the computer's main memory work space but returns the current program name.

In other versions of BASIC, the command NEW is used to clear the current contents of the computer's main memory. Usually, no other action occurs, and the computer returns to the READY or similar prompt.

In other words, after a NEW or SCRATCH, it's all gone! Be sure, therefore, to save a copy of any program you may want—before clearing the memory.

● **Sequential Data File:** A sequential data file is a list of data stored in the order it is written on the storage device. The storage device is usually a disk, and the file is called a disk file.

Retrieval of the data is also done sequentially, that is, from the first record to the last. If an item is to be retrieved from the middle of the file, all items up to the one sought must be "read through" first. The process of reading through does not delete the items from the storage.

As with random files, the process for reading items usually requires a sequence of statements in the BASIC program—OPEN, INPUT, and CLOSE. For the computer to read the file correctly, the arguments of these statements for sequential files are different from those used for random files.

The process for writing an item or a list of items to a sequential file usually requires a similar group of statements—OPEN, WRITE or PRINT, and CLOSE. Again, the arguments of these statements are different from the arguments for writing to a random file.

Think of the sequential file as a list. If an item is added to the list, it always goes at the end of the list. If an item is read from the list, the reading process always starts at the beginning of the list and proceeds toward the end. In this way, retrieval from a sequential file is nearly always slower than from a random file. Sequential files are often easier to create than random files, and they work well for small amounts of data where search time is not a problem.

• **Sequential Data File Creation:** Creating a sequential data file usually involves simply the statements OPEN, WRITE or PRINT, and CLOSE. If more than one data item is to be written, the WRITE or PRINT statement may be used inside a FOR-NEXT loop.

Some of the variations among the different versions of BASIC for the statements needed to create a sequential file are:

OPEN CMD INPUT INPUT# INPUT$
LINE INPUT# CLOSE LOC EOF LOF

Each of these statements may have from one to four (sometimes more) arguments.

• **Sequential Data File Reading:** In most applications, the information or data stored in a sequential data file will be read and then processed by a BASIC program. The data items in a sequential data file must be read in the same order that they are stored in, starting at the beginning of the sequential data file.

Note: All the information that is read will be retained for subsequent use.

The statements LOF and/or EOF are used to detect the end of the file so the computer doesn't try to read nonexisting data.

The keyword OPEN (or a variation, CMD) usually has as one of its arguments the assignment of a channel through which the computer will pass the data read. Another standard argument is the name of the file to be read.

The keyword INPUT (or its variations, INPUT#, INPUT$, or READ) moves a copy of the data item(s) into the buffer selected in the OPEN statement. The data can then be displayed on the screen, printed, or altered.

EXAMPLE:
```
10  OPEN "0",1,"DATES"
20  INPUT#1, K,J$,Z
30  PRINT K,J$,Z
40  IF EOF(1) THEN 60
50  GOTO 20
60  END
```

● **Sequential Data File Writing:** A BASIC program may write information onto a data file, much in the same manner as information is read from a sequential data file. Because sequential data files *are* sequential, new information or data will automatically be written beyond any existing data. This obviously protects any information already stored.

If the old data is to be deleted prior to the writing of new data, then the old data file must explicitly be erased and repositioned to its starting point.

The most often used statements in writing to a sequential data file are OPEN, PRINT, and CLOSE. Here is a list of variations:

Statement	Variations
OPEN	CMD
PRINT	PRINT#, WRITE#, PRINT USING
CLOSE	CMD

In addition, the keywords EOF and LOF usually keep track of the number of items in a sequential file and the length of the file in storage units respectively.

The OPEN statement must precede any other file manipulation statement. Its arguments usually specify the data channel (or buffer), the filename, and, for sequential files, the type of operation to be done—input or output. Once the buffer number has been stated, the data will be placed into the buffer area, then written to the storage unit. References to the buffer number are contained in the PRINT statement argument, not the file name. Therefore, the buffer assignment can be thought of as the link between the PRINT statement and the file being written to.

EXAMPLE:
```
10   OPEN "I",3,"SALES"
20   PRINT#3, D,M,R
30   CLOSE
```

Line 10 tells the computer three things: the I signals input to the file (the file will be written to); the 3 names the buffer through which all data will pass on its way to storage, and the file to which the data is to be written, SALES, is identified by its name.

In line 20, PRINT#3 informs the computer that the following data list, D, M, and R$, is to be written to buffer number 3. Because of the relations given in the preceeding OPEN statement, the computer will store data written to buffer 3 in the file SALES.

● **SET:** The SET statement is usually used to set different modes of operation within the BASIC interpreter or compiler. The following are examples of different modes that are affected by the SET statement.

1) SET RADIAN: sets trigonometric functions to radian mode.
2) SET DEGREE: sets trigonometric functions to degree mode.
3) SET GRAD: sets trigonometric functions to grad mode.
4) SET TRACE: sets trace mode, which in most versions of BASIC prints out the line numbers as they are being executed. This function is very useful in debugging.
5) SET NORMAL: cancels the SET TRACE function.

Of course, depending on the version of BASIC being used, there may or may not be SET statements, or different ones than those shown here.

EXAMPLE:

```
10    SET RADIANS
20    Y COS(X)
30    SET DEGREE
40    Z COS(X)
50    SET GRAD
60    K COS(X)
```

See also *Random Files Pointer Control.*

● **Set Pointer:** See *Random Data Files Pointer Control.*

● **SGN:** The library function SGN returns a one if the argument is positive (greater than zero); a zero if the argument is equal to zero, and minus one if the argument is negative (less than zero).

EXAMPLE:

```
10    PRINT SGN(10)
20    PRINT SGN(0)
```

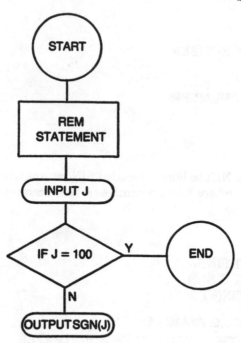

Flowchart for SGN function.

```
30    PRINT SGN(-45)
40    PRINT SGN(K*J)
```

PROGRAMMING EXAMPLE:

```
10    REM THIS PROGRAM DEMONSTRATES
20    REM THE SGN FUNCTION
30    PRINT "ENTER ANY NUMBER"
40    INPUT J
50    IF J = 100 THEN 80
60    PRINT SGN(J)
70    GOTO 30
80    END
```

RUN

ENTER ANY NUMBER
?0
0
ENTER ANY NUMBER

?-234
-1
ENTER ANY NUMBER
?28
1
ENTER ANY NUMBER
?100

END

● **SIN:** The library function SIN returns the sine of the expression X, where X is in parentheses. X is interpreted as being in radians.

EXAMPLE:
```
10    PRINT SIN(J)
20    PRINT SIN(Q)
30    Q = SIN(K)
```

PROGRAMMING EXAMPLE:
```
10    REM THIS PROGRAM DEMONSTRATES
20    REM THE SIN FUNCTION
```

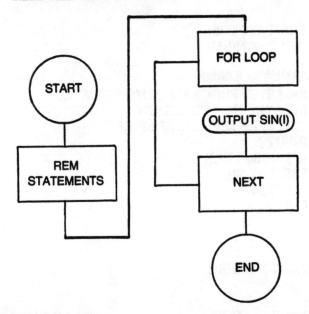

Flowchart for SIN function.

```
30    FOR I = 1 TO 5
40    PRINT SIN(I)
50    NEXT I
60    END
```

RUN

```
0.84147
0.90929
0.14112
-0.75680
-0.95892
```

END

● **Slash:** See *Colon.*

● **Space (Available):** To check how much relative space you have available for programs try the following program:

```
10    DIM J(K)
20    FOR I = 1 TO K
30    LET J(I) = J(I) + 1
40    NEXT I
50    END
```

Try different values of K until you receive a "OUT OF MEMORY" error message.

Other BASICs have statements which return either the amount of free space available to the programmer, or the amount of free string storage space. See *FRE.*

● **SPACE$:** The SPACE$ Function returns a string of spaces, the length being specified by the numeric formula, constant, or variable (truncated to an integer) in parentheses following the keyword SPACE$.

EXAMPLE:

```
10    SPACE$(10)
20    SPACE$(J)
30    SPACE$(J*K)
```

A related function is found in some BASICs, with the keyword SPC. It is used to skip spaces in a PRINT statement: PRINT "A";SPC(20);"B". This statement will print the letter A, skip 20 spaces, and print the letter B.

● **SQR:** The library function SQR returns the square root of the argument in parentheses. X must be greater than or equal to zero.

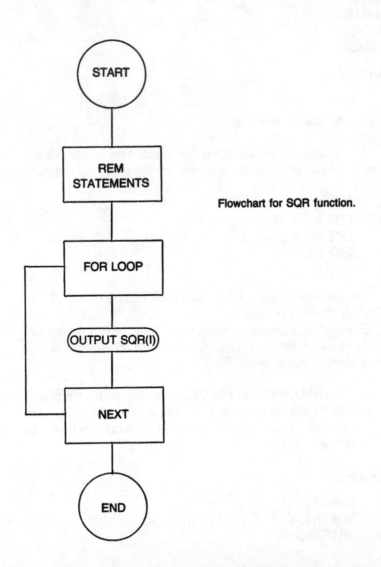

Flowchart for SQR function.

EXAMPLE:

```
10      PRINT SQR(Q)
20      K = SQR(J)
```

PROGRAMMING EXAMPLE:

```
10      REM THIS PROGRAM DEMONSTRATES
20      REM THE SQR FUNCTION
30      FOR I = 10 TO 100 STEP 10
40      PRINT SQR(I)
50      NEXT I
60      END
```

RUN

```
3.16227
4.47214
5.47722
6.32456
7.07107
7.74597
8.36667
8.94427
9.48683
10.0000
```

END

● **STATUS:** The STATUS or STA command is usually associated with large computer systems. After the user types in the STATUS command during command mode, the computer will respond with the following:

   A) The current program name.
   B) The current data and time.
   C) The amount of CPU time the user has used since LOGON.

   ● **STEP:** See *FOR-TO*.

   ● **STOP:** The STOP statement is used in BASIC to halt program execution. In effect it is a GOTO statement to the END statement.
   The STOP statement can be used more than once and anywhere within the structure of a program.

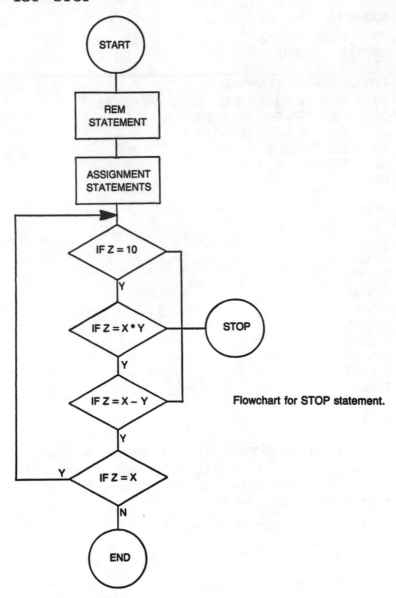

Flowchart for STOP statement.

PROGRAMMING EXAMPLE:

```
10    REM THIS PROGRAM DEMONSTRATES THE STOP
20    REM STATEMENT
30    LET Z = 10
40    LET X = 5
```

```
50    LET Y = 2
60    IF Z = 10 THEN 80
70    STOP   *
80    IF Z = X Y THEN 100
90    STOP
100   IF Z = X  Y THEN 120
110   STOP
120   IF Z = X THEN 60
130   END
```

● **STR$:** The library function STR$ returns a string which is the character representation of the numeric expression X.

The conversion of a numeric variable or number allows string operations to be performed on the value of either. In BASIC, a number usually has a blank space before it or after it, called a *leading blank* or *trailing blank*, to allow room for a minus sign, if needed. When printing a number, in order to line up a column, converting the number to a string can make it possible to eliminate this blank. See lines 20 and 30 of the following example.

Also, the STR$ statement can be used in counting the number of digits in a number. See line 40. Don't forget that the leading or trailing blank also adds to the length of the string.

EXAMPLE:

```
10    PRINT STR$(18.9)
20    D$ = RIGHT$(STR$(66), LEN(STR$(66)) - 1)
30    F$ = LEFT$(STR$(N), LEN (STR$(N)) - 1)
40    ND = LEN(STR$(45.6)) - 1
```

● **String:** A string is a sequence of characters (alphanumeric plus special characters such as +, −, /, *, $ . . . etc.). A blank space may be included in a string, but never quotation marks because quotation marks are delimiters and mark the beginning and the end of a string. The maximum number of characters any string may have will depend on the version of BASIC being used. The function of a string is to represent such nonnumeric data as labels, messages, etc.

Note: A sequence of integers in a string does not represent a numeric data.

Sometimes it is desirable to print a quotation mark (not an apostrophe, but the double quote mark) either on the screen or on

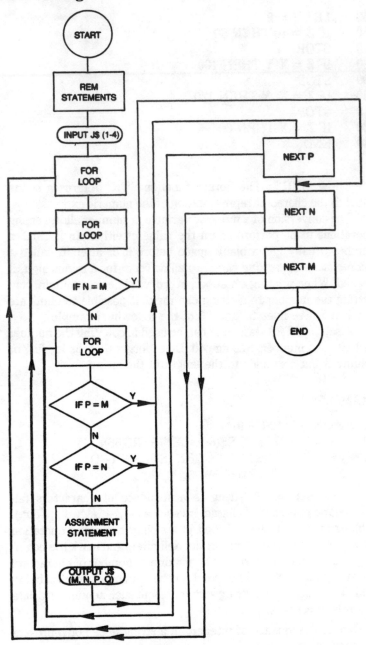

Flowchart for String manipulation.

the printer. In this case, a little trick is needed. Instead of writing PRINT " " ", which will get you some very odd results indeed, notice that the ASCII code for the double quote mark is 34. Write PRINT CHR$(34) wherever the double quote mark is needed, and it will appear.

EXAMPLES:
"BASIC"
"THIS IS A STRING"
"THE DATE IS"
"TYPE YES TO RESTART"
"$153.92"
"301019491621959"

PROGRAMMING EXAMPLE:
```
10    REM THIS PROGRAM DEMONSTRATES STRING
20    REM MANIPULATION
30    PRINT "TYPE ANY FOUR LETTERS"
40    INPUT J$(1),J$(2),J$(3),J$(4)
50    FOR M = 1 TO 4
60    FOR N = 1 TO 4
70    IF N = M THEN 140
80    FOR P = 1 TO 4
90    IF P = M THEN 130
100   IF P = N THEN 130
110   LET R = 10-(M + N + P)
120   PRINT J$(M); J$(N); J$(P); J$(R)
130   NEXT P
140   NEXT N
150   NEXT M
160   END
```

● **Subroutines:** A subroutine is a program within a program that does a predefined function. Sometimes it is easier and more useful to structure such a procedure as a subroutine than as a function. Subroutines, like functions, may be referenced from different points within a program. Whereas a function is given a name, a subroutine is not; it is referenced by the line number of the first statement of the subroutine. A subroutine can determine more than one numeric and/or string quantity, and arguments are not required. Thus a subroutine may be viewed as a very generalized function.

A subroutine may be called from different points in the program by the GOSUB and the ON-GOSUB commands. The first statement within the subroutine structure may be of any type, but the last statement must always be the keyword RETURN. A subroutine may have more than one RETURN statement, as for multiple or conditional branching procedures.

The advantage of the subroutine structure is the ability to write a section of code once, yet use it in many places in the same program, which saves a lot of memory, especially if the subroutine is large, and it is called several times. If a subroutine contains 10 lines of statements and is called six times, we can save 38 lines of code. Why 38? Every subroutine must end in a return statement; thus the routine itself is only nine lines long. We have six call statements, nine lines of routine, and one return, or 16 lines total. If all nine lines had been written six times throughout the program, 54 lines would have been required.

In some of the newer BASICs, named subroutines are available. In this type, the computer must first be given the name of the subroutine and its location. Then the subroutine may be invoked by the GOSUB name statement instead of the usual GOSUB line. The following example shows the use of these statements

EXAMPLE:

```
10     SAMPLESUB = 5200
  .
  .
  .
300    GOSUB SAMPLESUB
  .
  .
  .
5200 X = 27*T: REM THIS IS THE FIRST LINE OF
SAMPLESUB
  .
  .
  .
5300 RETURN: REM THIS IS THE LAST LINE OF
SAMPLESUB
```

● **Subscripted Variables:** The individual elements within an array are known as subscripted variables. Any element in an array can be referred to by using the array name followed by the value of the subscript in parentheses. With lists, only one subscript is required; with tables, two subscripts are needed to properly identify any given element.

The subscripts may be variables, numbers, or formulas. The following are valid subscript variables:

K(J)
L(M)
H(1,5)
Z(K1, J1)
P(ABS(X-4), ABS(X + 4))

Note: The variable, or formula written within the parentheses, will be truncated if it has a value that is noninteger. If the value is negative, an error message will be generated, and program execution will be halted.

Subscript variables may be used as ordinary variables within a program.

By placing subscript variables within loops and using either counter techniques or the FOR-TO loop technique, we can refer to the elements in the array with ease. **Note:** Remember the running variable of the FOR-TO statement may be used within the loop as long as its value is not changed.

● **System Commands:** See *User Commands.*

● **TAB:** The library function TAB spaces to a specified position on the printer or video terminal. It must be used in conjunction with a PRINT statement. The TAB function specifies the absolute position from the left-hand margin where printing is to start.

EXAMPLE:
```
10    PRINT TAB(J)
```

PROGRAMMING EXAMPLE:
```
10    REM THIS PROGRAM DEMONSTRATES
20    REM THE TAB FUNCTION
30    FOR I = 1 TO 5
40    PRINT TAB(J)"BASIC"
50    NEXT I
60    END
```

RUN

BASIC
 BASIC
  BASIC
   BASIC
    BASIC

END

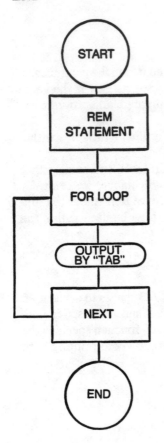

Flowchart for TAB function.

● **TAN:** The library function TAN returns the tangent of the argument in parentheses, interpreted as being in radians.

EXAMPLE:

```
10    PRINT TAN(J)
20    K = TAN(J)
```

PROGRAMMING EXAMPLE:

```
10    REM THIS PROGRAM DEMONSTRATES
20    REM THE TAN FUNCTION
30    FOR I = 1 TO 5
40    PRINT TAN(I)
50    NEXT I
60    END
```

RUN

1.55741
-2.18503
-0.14254
1.15782
-3.38052

END

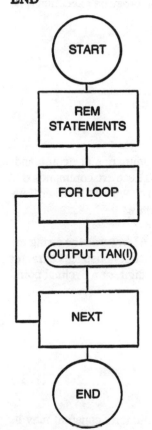

Flowchart for TAN function.

● **TEXT:** The TEXT or TEX command is used in conjunction with the versions of BASIC that have graphics capabilities. The command TEXT sets the video output back to standard text mode (alphanumerics plus the standard symbols).

● **THEN:** See *GOTO*.

● **TIM:** To find the amount of time required to run a program, the TIM function may be used. The TIM function requires a dummy argument in parentheses. The value given by TIM is processor time, in seconds, used since the RUN command was given to the computer.

In other versions of BASIC, the function may be named TIME$ or TI$. To time a program, use a line like: B$ = TIME$ at the beginning of the program, and: E$ = TIME$ at the end. Then, by printing out and comparing the two, the program execution time may be calculated.

EXAMPLE:

10   PRINT "TIME = "; TIM(X)

● **USER:** See *CALL*.

● **User Commands:** User Commands are commands such as RUN, LOAD, SAVE, and LIST. These are commands that are independent of the program being run concurrently. User Commands are often termed *System Commands*.

● **VAL:** The library function VAL returns the string expression X$ converted to a number. If the first nonspace character of the string is not a plus or minus sign, a digit, or a decimal point, then a zero will be returned.

EXAMPLE:

10   PRINT VAL(J$)
20   PRINT VAL("123.4")   (123.4)

● **VARIABLES:** A string or numeric constant may be

represented by a name called a variable. In most versions of BASIC each numeric variable must consist of a letter or a letter followed by an integer. A string variable must be written as a letter followed by a dollar sign, ($).

Most versions of BASIC allow only two characters at most to identify a variable name. More than two characters may be used, but the added ones are ignored by the computer. In this case, the variables VO and VOTE would be considered identical, as would the string variables GA$ and GAME$.

Other versions of BASIC consider up to 40 characters valid.

Be careful not to use a keyword as a variable name. Most versions of BASIC do not allow you to do so. For example, don't use PRINT as the name of a variable.

EXAMPLES:

$$I \quad J \quad K1 \quad J2 \quad X4 \quad Z9$$

$$I\$ \quad J\$ \quad K1 \quad J2\$ \quad X4\$ \quad Z9$$

COUNTER$ AC$ DOT$ ADDRESS$ XY

PARTNO   PN   YPOS   FLAG   GG

● **Vector and Matrix Operations:** MATRIX and VECTOR are mathematical terms that are in reference to a table and a list respectively. A one-dimensional array is called a vector, while a two-dimensional array is termed a matrix. A vector is therefore only a special type of matrix, and thus most of the rules that apply to matrices apply to vectors.

The individual elements of the array are represented by subscript variables. When dealing with matrices the subscript variable required two subscripts, for example $J(K,L)$, where K represents the row and L the column. Thus $J(5,8)$ is the element found in the fifth row and eighth column of the matrix J. If a matrix has K rows and L columns, it is referred to as a K-×-L matrix.

In most versions of BASIC, a subscript has a preset value of 10. If a greater value is required, a DIM statement must be used.

The operations in addition, subtraction, scalar multiplication, and vector multiplication are the most common vector and matrix operations.

Appendix

Appendix

DERIVED FUNCTIONS

The following functions which are not typical of standard BASIC library functions may be easily implemented by the following formulas:

```
ARC SIN(×) = ATN(×/SQR(1 - × * ×))
ARC COS(×) = 1.5708 - ATN(×/SQR(1 - × * ×))
ARC SEC(X) = ATN(SQR(X*X - 1)) + (SGN(X) - 1)*1.5708
ARC CSC(X) = ATN(1/SQR(X*X) - 1)) + (SGN(X) - 1)*1.5708
ARC COT(X) = -ATN(X) + 1.5708
ARC SINH(X) = LOG(X + SQR(X*X + 1))
ARC COSII(X) = LOG(X + SQR(X*X - 1))
ARC TANH(X) = LOG((1 + X)/(1 - X))/2
ARC SECH(×) = LOG((SQR(1 - × * ×) + 1)/×)
ARC CSCH(X) = LOG((SGN(X)*SQR(X*X + 1) + 1)/X)
ARC COTH(×) = LOG((× + 1)/(× - 1))/2
COT(X) = 1/TAN(X)
CSC(X) = 1/SIN(X)
SEC(X) = 1/COS(X)
COSH(X) = (EXP(X) + EXP(- X))/2
COTH(X) = EXP(-X)/(EXP(X) - EXP(- X))*2 + 1
CSCH(X) = 2/(EXP(X) - EXP(-X))
SECH(×) = 2/(ESP(×) + EXP (×))
SINH(X) = (EXP(X) - EXP(-X))/2
TANH(X) = -EXP(-X)/(EXP(X) + EXP(-X))*2 + 1
```

DIAGNOSTICS (COMMON)

READ/RESUME, NO DATA: The user has not provided any DATA statement or data but has used either the READ or RESTORE statements.

FOR, NO NEXT: The user has constructed a FOR-TO loop but has not closed it with a NEXT statement.

UNDIMENSIONED: Variables that were being used as matrices were not dimensioned.

VECTOR + ARRAY: The same variable was used both as a vector and an array.

VALUE OUTSIDE RANGE: A value has exceeded the bounds for that particular function.

GOSUB NESTING: The user has used more levels of GOSUB nesting than the version of BASIC used allows.

RETURN: A RETURN statement was executed before a GOSUB statement.

DIVISION BY ZERO: Division by zero was tried.

INVALID EXPONENT: A**B, where A<0 and B<>INT (B).

LOG(–X): The log of a negative number was specified.

SQR(–X): The square root of a negative number was specified.

OUT OF DATA: The set of DATA elements has been exhausted and a READ statement is executed.

ILLEGAL CONSTANT: A string (numeric) data element is read into a numeric (string) variable.

FUNCTION PREVIOUSLY DEFINED: A user-defined function (DEF statement) has been defined more than once in one program.

ARRAY PREVIOUSLY DIMENSIONED: An array or a matrix has been defined more than once in one program.

NO SUCH LINE#: A reference has been made to a nonexistent line number.

FOR NESTING (MAX = X): Where the user has exceeded the maximum of nesting (where X is the maximum for that particular version of BASIC).

NESTING SAME INDEX: Where a user has constructed a nested FOR loop with two or more of the FOR-TO statements using the same running variable (index variable).

WRONG NEXT: The matching NEXT statement must follow the corresponding FOR-TO statement.

ILLEGAL NESTING: FOR-TO loops may be nested, but they must not overlap.

OVERFLOW: A numeric constant exceeds the maximum single-precision floating-point value.

UNDERFLOW: A numeric constant is smaller than the minimum single-precision floating-point value.

MEMORY EXCEEDED: The generated object code exceeds the bounds permitted by the computer and/or the version of BASIC being used.

INCREASE PROGRAM SPEED

1) Use GOSUB sparingly.
2) Minimize GOTOs from one section to another section of the program.
3) Check if FOR-NEXT is faster than or slower than IF-THEN loops.
4) For simpler integer multiplication, such as 2*K, K + K will be faster.
5) Check whether simple code is faster than or slower than complex expressions.

SAVING SPACE

To conserve space and limit the size of programs the following hints may be implemented.

A) Use multiple statements per line number, if the version of BASIC allows. There is an overhead of about 5 bytes associated with each line in a program.
B) Use integer values whenever possible as opposed to real numbers.
C) Delete all unnecessary spaces from program lines.

EXAMPLE:

```
10   PRINT K, J; L
```

Could be entered as

```
10   PRINTK,J;L
```

D) Use as few REM statements as possible.
E) Use variables rather than constants, when the same constant is required more than a few times.
F) A program that is one loop and is ended by either CTRL-C or by running out of data usually does not require an END statement.

G) Re-use variables over and over if possible.

H) Use GOSUBs instead of repeating lines of code.

SPEED (Processing)

The following program may be timed to give an indication of processing speed.

```
10    FOR I = 1 TO 1000
20    LET X = X+1
30    NEXT I
40    PRINT X
50    END
```

Instead of line 20 being LET X = X+1, the user may try 20 LETX = 10*X or 20 LETX = X/10. Multiplication and division are fairly complex software routines. Using these two replacements will give a fair indication of this type of operation speed.